The Immigration Solution

The Immigration Solution

A Better Plan Than Today's

HEATHER MAC DONALD

VICTOR DAVIS HANSON

STEVEN MALANGA

Ivan R. Dee   Chicago   2007

THE IMMIGRATION SOLUTION. Copyright © 2007 by the Manhattan Institute. All rights reserved, including the right to reproduce this book or portions thereof in any form. For information, address: Ivan R. Dee, Publisher, 1332 North Halsted Street, Chicago 60622. Manufactured in the United States of America and printed on acid-free paper.

www.ivanrdee.com

Most of the contents of this book appeared originally in *City Journal*, published by the Manhattan Institute.

Library of Congress Cataloging-in-Publication Data:
Mac Donald, Heather.
   The immigration solution : a better plan than today's /
Heather Mac Donald, Victor Davis Hanson, Steven Malanga.
       p. cm.
   Includes index.
   ISBN-13: 978-1-56663-760-2 (cloth : alk. paper)
   ISBN-10: 1-56663-760-0 (cloth : alk. paper)
   1. Illegal aliens—United States—Social conditions. 2. Mexicans—United States—Social conditions. 3. Immigrants—Government policy—United States. 4. Mexico—Emigration and immigration.
I. Hanson, Victor Davis. II. Malanga, Steven. III. Title.
JV6483.M25 2007
325'.2720973—dc22

                                                          2007012768

Contents

The Immigration Solution

Introduction

MYRON MAGNET

T*he Immigration Solution* argues that America needs a liberal and welcoming immigration policy, geared above all to the needs and interests of our own nation. Formulating such a policy requires at the outset changing the terms of today's immigration debate.

Currently, to be "pro-immigration" means that you support the status quo, in which we have lost control of our southern border, so that the vast majority of our immigrants are Mexicans, most of them here illegally. Self-proclaimed pro-immigration advocates support one or another form of amnesty for these illegals, claiming that despite their status they are a boon to the U.S. economy, which needs them to do "jobs that Americans won't do." In addition, the advocates contend, our eleven million–plus illegal Mexican immigrants strengthen U.S. society with their upright family values and powerful work ethic.

Neither of these claims withstands scrutiny, as the following chapters show. As for the economic argument, Steven Malanga demonstrates in Chapter 2 that the U.S. economy is not crying out for unskilled workers—and most Mexican migrants are unskilled. These workers are already in such oversupply in America that they have a higher rate of unemployment than other workers and are pushing down one another's wages. When immigration authorities raided six Swift & Co. meatpacking plants and detained undocumented workers in December 2006, for example, the line of applicants for their now-vacant jobs stretched out the door at some plants, and job seekers questioned by reporters showed proof of U.S. citizenship. When a Colorado construction company boss complained on network news that same month that he couldn't find American citizens who would take entry-level jobs, he had e-mail applications waiting for him when his TV appearance ended, and six hundred hopefuls telephoned within the next few days.

While the cheapness of the immigrants' labor may benefit a very few industries and provide some upper- and middle-class families with cut-rate gardeners and nannies, it adds very little to our national standard of living. On the other side of the ledger, the costs these immigrants impose on U.S. taxpayers for health care, schooling, welfare, and (all too often) incarceration far outweigh the benefits they offer. In California, the National Academy of Sciences found, immigrant families cost each native-born household an additional $1,200 in taxes per year. To put it another way, Robert Rector of the Heritage Foundation calculates that each immigrant who is a high school dropout, as most Mexican immigrants are, will end up costing taxpayers some $85,000 over his lifetime.

Although a net loss for the United States, such workers are an unalloyed boon for Mexico. Their ability to find work north of the border is an essential safety valve for Mexico's failed economy and stubbornly unreformed political culture, and the remittances these workers send home are indispensable to Mexico, constituting its second-largest source of hard currency. No wonder the Mexican government—especially through its consuls in the United States—vigorously fosters the illegal migration of its nationals into its northern neighbor. As Heather Mac Donald shows in Chapter 7, these diplomats constantly engage in a most undiplomatic interference in U.S. internal affairs on behalf of their illegal countrymen.

Pro-immigration free marketers believe that labor should be able to move around the globe as freely as capital. At its extreme, theirs is an argument that nations should have no sovereignty over their own borders. These free marketers see labor as fungible, like capital—a worker is a worker, fit for any slot where the economy offers opportunity. Not so, Steven Malanga warns. Workers are individuals, with their own views and values—and low-skilled Hispanic immigrants and their U.S.-born children present a conundrum that for decades troubled observers of the urban underclass: in an economy teeming with opportunity, where all you need for success is to grab the free education the state offers, why do some groups stay mired in poverty? The answer is a group culture that devalues education and assimilation and that overvalues early childbearing (whether in wedlock or not) and a brittle, exaggerated male pride—exactly the culture that the biggest portion of today's immigrants bring with them.

Heather Mac Donald vividly fleshes out this theme in Chapters 3 through 6. If amnesty advocates would actually examine the facts on the ground and trust reports from local communities, they would see that today's unskilled Hispanic immigrants—anti-education, anti-assimilationist, even anti–English language—are becoming a new underclass, living in ethnic enclaves that are ridden with crime, violent gangs, drug dealing, illegitimacy, school failure, welfare dependency, and poverty. Just at the moment when America's underclass problem looked soluble, that class has received vast reinforcements, harder to assimilate and bound to spark a welfare-state boom, with new hordes of don't-blame-the-victim functionaries. (Thus when conservatives say these immigrants might increasingly become new Republican voters, one recalls the old immigrant joke about the manufacturer whose bad news was that he was losing a nickel on every item he sold. The good news? He was going to make it up on volume.)

The result of these developments for the quality of life in local communities has been catastrophic, as Victor Davis Hanson, a lifetime resident of California's heavily Mexican San Joaquin Valley, recounts. Hanson went to school with Mexican friends, saw his relatives and children marry Mexicans, and watched Mexicans assimilate wholeheartedly into American culture. Now everything has changed, in what Californians have begun to call the "Invasion." The original crime of illegal entry breeds more crime and disorder, so that longtime residents increasingly find their property vandalized or burgled. They get into traffic accidents with uninsured drivers, see newcomers illegally crowding into housing and flouting sanitary regulations, and live with the sense that the security of their world has collapsed. The prevalence of Spanish in the shops and schools intensifies their uneasy feeling that the communities they helped build have been taken away from them. And the growing political radicalism and Mexican chauvinism of the newcomers raise faint but troubling echoes of the sectarian strife that has convulsed the Middle East and exploded Yugoslavia.

Some advocates argue that the Mexican immigrants' wan economic performance, along with their high levels of criminality, illegitimacy, and illiteracy, results solely from their outlaw status. Legalize them through an amnesty, the argument goes, and all will be well. But such a contention—which mirrors earlier rationalizations that underclass social pathology springs from racism and injustice, and that to hold underclass criminals responsible for their actions is unfairly to "blame the victim" when in fact the larger society is to blame—founders on the fact that the legal children of Mexican immigrants have such high dropout and unemployment rates. Instead of explaining the reality we see, such an argument is merely an attempt to explain it away.

You might counter that so harsh an assessment of the new immigrants is the kind of claptrap that prejudiced nativists used to spout during the first great migration into America. They liked to jeer that Eastern European Jewish immigrants tested subnormal on intelligence tests, you might point out, and that Italians took generations to reach solidly middle-class levels of education and income—but reach them they most certainly did in America's land of opportunity and freedom. No one is more sensitive to such objections than the staff of *City Journal*, where the chapters of this book first appeared. We publish from the great immigrant metropolis, lit by the Statue of Liberty's torch, under which many of our forebears passed. We know what our city, our nation, and we ourselves owe to immigrants. And watching today's Hispanic newcomers on their delivery bikes in the snow or on high building-repair scaffolds in the summer heat, who can't share President Bush's belief that these are good, hardworking people who deserve a chance?

But those earlier huddled masses of immigrants yearning to breathe free, however tired and poor they may have looked, were in fact on average *more* skilled than the native-born population of a century ago. In addition, the less-developed economy of that era also had a vastly greater need for immigrants without skills than does today's knowledge economy. More important, the U.S. immigration system of that period was a machine for selecting the most enterprising and energetic migrants. With no welfare system whatever, those who came were those who thought they could make use of the opportunity and freedom America offered by their own efforts. Grateful for the chance, these newcomers were only too glad to assimilate to their new land as best they could, and their children did so wholeheartedly.

Not so today. The first child born in America to an immigrant entitles his or her family to child-only welfare payments—a hefty-looking sum to a recent migrant from a peasant village. Moreover, instead of being encouraged to assimilate, and instructed how to do it, by the settlement houses and self-help associations of yore, today's Hispanic immigrants hear only a message of ethnic separateness and chauvinism from organizations like La Raza and other immigrant advocacy groups. Unlike the militantly assimilationist public schools that trained earlier generations of immigrants to be Americans, today's schools, worshipping at the multiculturalist shrine and wedded to bilingual education, encourage immigrant kids to cling to their Hispanic identity, and they teach them at least as much about the injustices done by their new country as about the unexampled degree of freedom, prosperity, and tolerance it has achieved. While pro-immigration advocates may argue that all we need to do is assimilate our immigrants, we would need a wholesale reformation of our culture and our welfare regulations to do so.

No one is suggesting that we round up all our illegals and deport them. Instead, what these pages do urge is that we simply enforce existing law, policing our border vigorously and fining employers who hire illegals. Deprived of work, illegals would return home, just as 60 percent of immigrants from the first great migration eventually left these shores when they couldn't make it here.

Instead of passively accepting the state of affairs that our lax enforcement and the unlawful behavior of so many immigrants has brought about, which threatens enormous and untoward consequences for our society and economy, we should be determining our own destiny. We should be crafting a new immigration policy similar to

those of other advanced democracies that are also immigrant magnets. Generous in the numbers of newcomers it
admits, our new policy should select newcomers not because they are someone's brother or adult child or elderly
parents, or because they successfully sneaked into the
country some years ago, but because they have some special skill, from stonecutting to auto mechanics to electri-
cal engineering, that will enrich our nation. The world is
teeming with people who want to come to America to benefit from the free and prosperous society that our forebears have constructed and to which we citizens have
ourselves contributed. Since we can only take a small frac-
tion of prospective migrants, surely it is right to ask what
immigrants can do for our country, not what our country
can do for them.

NOTE TO THE READER

The chapters that follow, substantially altered, first appeared in *City Journal* in the following years:

1

VICTOR DAVIS HANSON

Do We Want Mexifornia?

Thousands arrive illegally from Mexico into California each year—and the state is now home to fully 40 percent of America's immigrants, legal and illegal. They come in such numbers because a tacit alliance of Right and Left has created an open-borders policy, aimed at keeping wage labor cheap and social problems ever fresh, so that the ministrations of Chicano studies professors, La Raza ("The Race") activists, and all the other self-appointed defenders of group causes will never be unneeded. The tragedy is that though illegal aliens come here hoping to succeed, most get no preparation for California's competitive culture. Instead, their activist shepherds herd them into ethnic enclaves, where inexorably they congeal into an underclass. The concept of multiculturalism is the force multiplier that produces this result: it transforms a stubborn problem of assimilation into a social calamity.

Given hard feelings over recent ballot initiatives that curtailed not only aid to illegals but also affirmative action and bilingual education, unlawful immigration has become the third rail of California politics. Even to discuss the issue can earn politicians the cheap slander of "racist" or "nativist." Tensions abound even within families. One of my siblings is married to a Mexican American; another has two stepchildren whose father was an illegal alien from Mexico; I have a prospective son-in-law whose parents crossed the border. Yet we all disagree at different times whether open borders are California's hope or its bane.

And why not? Californians cannot even obtain accurate numbers of how many of the state's more than 10 million Hispanic residents have arrived here from Mexico unlawfully in the last two decades. No one believes the government's old insistence on a mere 6 million illegal residents nationwide; the real figure may be twice that. The U.S. Hispanic population—of which more than 70 percent are from Mexico—grew 53 percent during the 1980s, and then rose another 27 percent to a total of 30 million between 1990 and 1996. At present rates of births and immigration, by 2050 there will be 97 million Hispanics, one-quarter of the American population.

Nor is there agreement on the economic effects of the influx. Liberal economists swear that legal immigrants to America bring in $25 billion in net revenue annually. More skeptical statisticians using different models conclude that aliens cost the United States more than $40 billion a year, and that here in California each illegal immigrant will take $50,000 in services from the state beyond what he will contribute in taxes during his lifetime. Other studies suggest that the average California household must contribute at least $1,200 each year to subsidize the deficit between what immigrants cost in services and pay in taxes.

The irony, of course, is that the present immigration crisis was not what any Californian had anticipated. Along with the cheap labor that the tax-conscious Right wanted, it got thousands of unassimilated others, who eventually flooded into the state's near-bankrupt entitlement industry and filled its newly built prisons: California is $12 billion in the red this year, and nearly one-quarter of its inmates are aliens from Mexico (while nearly a third of all drug-trafficking arrests involve illegal aliens). The pro-labor Left found that the industrious new arrivals whom it championed eroded the wages of its own domestic low-wage constituencies—the Labor Department attributes 50 percent of real-wage declines to the influx of cheap immigrant labor. And while the Democrats think the illegals will eventually turn into liberal voters, the actual Hispanic vote so far remains just a small fraction of the eligible Mexican-American pool: of the 14,173 residents of the central California town of Hanford who identified themselves as Latino (34 percent of the town's population), for example, only 770 are registered to vote.

My sleepy hometown of Selma, California, is in the dead center of all this. The once-rural San Joaquin Valley community has grown from seven thousand to nearly twenty thousand in a mere two decades, as a result of mostly illegal immigration from Mexico. Selma is now somewhere between 60 and 90 percent Hispanic. How many are U.S. citizens is either not known or not publicly disclosed: but of all those admitted *legally* from Mexico to the United States since 1982, only 20 percent had become citizens by 1997. Some local schools, like the one I went to two miles from our farm, are 90 percent first-generation Mexican immigrants. At the service station a mile away, I rarely hear English spoken; almost every car that pulls in displays a Mexican flag decal pasted somewhere.

To contrast the Selma I live in today with the Selma I grew up in will doubtless seem hopelessly nostalgic. But the point of the contrast is not merely that forty years ago our community was only 40 or 50 percent Mexican, but rather that the immigrants then were mostly here legally. Crime was far rarer: the hit-and-run accidents, auto theft, drug manufacturing and sale, murders, rapes, and armed robberies that are now customary were then nearly nonexistent. Fights that now end in semiautomatic-weapons fire were settled with knives then.

I used to worry over the theft of a tractor battery. Yet in the last decade I have run off at gunpoint three gang members trying to force their way into our house at 3 a.m. Last year four patrol cars—accompanied by a helicopter whirling overhead—chased drug dealers in hot pursuit through our driveway. One suspect escaped and turned up two hours later hiding behind a hedge on our lawn, vainly seeking sanctuary from a sure prison term. When a carload of thieves tried to steal oranges from our yard, I soon found myself outmanned and outgunned—and decided that one hundred pounds of pilfered fruit is not worth your life.

It is a schizophrenic existence, living at illegal immigration's intersection. Each week I pick up trash, dirty diapers, even sofas and old beds dumped in our orchard by illegal aliens—only to call a Mexican-American sheriff who empathizes when I show him the evidence of Spanish names and addresses on bills and letters scattered among the trash. So far I have caught more than fifteen illegal dumpers, all Mexican, in the act. In the last twenty years, four cars piloted by intoxicated illegal aliens have veered off the road into our vineyard, causing thousands of dollars in unrecompensed damage. The drivers simply limped away and disappeared. The police sighed, "No license, no insurance, no registration" ("the three noes"), and towed out their cars.

Yet I also walk through vineyards at 7 a.m. in the fog and see whole families from Mexico, hard at work in the cold—while the native-born unemployed of all races will not—and cannot—prune a single vine. By natural selection, we are getting some of the most intelligent and industrious people in the world, people who have the courage to cross the border, the tenacity to stay—and, if not assimilated, the potential to cost the state far, far more than they can contribute.

We know what caused the tidal waves of immigration of the last three decades. While Mexico's economy has been in a state of chronic collapse, California has needed workers of a certain type—muscular, uneducated, and industrious—to cut our lawns, harvest fruit, cook and serve meals, baby-sit kids, build homes, clean offices, and make beds in motels and nursing homes. The poor from Armenia, Japan, China, the Azores, and Oklahoma had all begun their odysseys of success in California doing just these menial tasks, albeit in far smaller numbers. But despite mechanization, California today demands more, not less, stoop work than thirty years ago, because of the state's radically changed attitudes and newly affluent lifestyle.

When I was ten, in 1963, all suburbanites mowed their own lawns—many with push mowers. Now almost everyone hires the job out. Nannies for toddlers and grannies, unheard-of then, are now ubiquitous from Visalia to Palos Verdes. Rural schools used to begin in mid-September to ensure that we natives could pick grapes to earn our school clothes and shoes. Today not a single student in California would do such hot, dirty work, now considered demeaning. With demand for such workers high and the supply of native-born citizens willing to do it low, Mexico came to the rescue of California.

There is a well-known cycle in California immigration. Young people between ages fifteen and thirty arrive here illegally and for a while stay single. Over decades, many live hard and toil at menial jobs, earning perhaps eight dollars an hour, usually paid in cash, which is a bargain for everyone involved. Without state, federal, and payroll taxes, the worker earns the equivalent of a gross ten-dollar-an-hour rate, while the employer saves 30 percent in payroll contributions, audits, and paperwork—even as such cash payments force other Americans and legal immigrants to pay steeper taxes, in part to cover those who don't pay. The immigrants work hard until their joints stiffen and their backs give out. By then their families are large. Their English stays perpetually poor; their education is still nonexistent, even as their IDs remain fraudulent.

Now, eight dollars per hour in California, rather than per week in Mexico, no longer seems such a bonanza, and they use their counterfeit documentation to get onto workers' compensation, unemployment insurance, and state assistance to garner what their weary bodies can no longer earn. Meanwhile they romanticize a distant Mexico while chastising an ever-present America. And the second generation has learned how to live, spend, and consume as Americans, but not, like their fathers, to work and save as Mexicans. If rising crime rates, gang activity, and illegitimacy are any indication, many now resent, rather than sacrifice to escape, their poverty. And the rates are rising fast: for example, while 37 percent of all births to Hispanic immigrants are illegitimate, the illegitimacy rate among American-born Mexican mothers is 48 percent.

Census data show us that median household income by the mid-1990s had risen for a decade for all groups, except for the nation's Hispanics, whose incomes dropped 5.1 percent. Although recent immigrants from Mexico and their U.S.-born children under eighteen now officially make up only 4.2 percent of America's population, they represent 10.2 percent of our poor. When you add in long-time residents, Hispanics account for 24 percent of America's impoverished, up 8 percentage points since 1985. The true causes of such checkered progress—continual and massive illegal immigration of cheap labor that drives down wages for working Hispanics here; failure to learn

English; the collapse of the once-strong Hispanic family due to federal entitlement; soaring birthrates among a demoralized underclass; an intellectual elite that downplays social pathology, claims perpetual racism, and seeks constant government largesse and entitlement; and years of bilingual education that ensure dependency upon a demagogic leadership—are rarely mentioned.

They cannot be mentioned. To do so would be to suggest that the billions of public dollars spent on social redress did more to harm Hispanics than did all the racists in America. Moreover, we wish to maintain cordial relations with Mexico—but in many ways no government in the last fifty years has been more hostile. Mexico's policy for a half-century has been the deliberate and illegal export of millions of its poorest citizens to the United States, which is expected to educate, employ, and protect them in ways not possible at home. Only that way has the chronically corrupt Mexican government avoided a revolution, as its exploited underclass from Oaxaca or the small hamlets of the Sierra Madre Mountains headed north, rather than marching en masse on Mexico City. Only that way can billions of earned foreign currency be sent home to prop up a bankrupt economy; only that way for the first time in his life can a poor Mixtec from Michoacan find an advocate for his health and safety from the Mexican consulate—once he is safely ensconced far north of the border.

You can leave Selma and be across the border in about six hours. That proximity in terms of immigration is paradoxical. The richest economy in the world is only a stone's throw from one of the most backward. The illegal alien leaves his pueblo in Yucatán, where cattle starve for adequate fodder, and in a day can be processed through familial connections to begin mowing and bagging fescue grass in the most leisured and affluent suburbs in Los Angeles.

Mexican Americans never experience the physical or psychological amputation from the mother country that most other immigrants to California found, after thousands of miles of seawater cut the old country clean off and relegated it to the romance of memory. But the Mexican immigrant can easily recross the Rio Grande by a drive over a short bridge. A limited annual visit or a family reunion nourishes enough nostalgia for Mexico to war with the creation of a truly American identity.

For Mexican immigrants, the idea of Mexico has shifted from a liability to an important benchmark of ethnic pride in the last two decades. A visiting Mexican soccer club playing almost any American team will find in our local fans a home-crowd advantage—despite being a thousand miles from home. Mexicans in California turn out to vote in booths set up in California for local and national candidates in Mexico, who come up to campaign in Fresno every year—and often learn to their dismay that California's Mexicans are among the sternest critics of Mexico City's endemic government corruption.

Instead of growing more distant, a romanticized Mexico stays close to the heart of the new arrival and turns into a roadblock on his journey to becoming an American. Many immigrants die as Mexicans in California, never seeking to become citizens. A columnist for our local paper recently described their suspension between two worlds: *"Pensaban que se iban a ir patria"* ("They thought they would go back"). Aside from our own self-interest in having our residents accept the responsibilities of full citizenship, it is entirely in the material interest of aliens to integrate and assimilate as quickly as possible into the general culture of California: they will eat better and have nicer houses and more secure futures for their children in California if they become Americans rather than permanent Mexican aliens.

Some sociologists and journalists assure us that retaining this cultural umbilical cord is not injurious. Instead we are creating a unique regional culture that is neither Mexican nor American but an amorphous, fluid society that is the dividend on our multicultural investment. This Calexico or Mexifornia will not be a bad thing at all but something, if not advantageous, at least inevitable. So we allow illegal aliens to obtain California driver's licenses—the foundation of all other means of legal identification—and to pay reduced in-state tuition at the University of California, thereby providing several thousand dollars in discounts not available to American citizens from out of state. Whether you break the law to reach California or immigrate legally, it makes little difference in how you drive, send your kids to college, or draw on the public services of the state.

These pundits hope privately, of course—though they do not say so publicly—that this new regional civilization will resemble San Diego more than Tijuana. And in truth, no immigrant, despite his grandiose boasts, wants to return to Mexico or anything like it, to be a Mexican in Mexico rather than in California.

And here we come to the heart of our immigration problem. It is not that our state is too crowded per se: Japan, after all, feeds, clothes, and educates three times as many as we Californians do, without our natural wealth or open spaces. The real problem is that, while it has always been easier for people who emigrate to keep their own culture rather than join the majority, for the first time in our state's (and nation's) history, the majority feels it is easier to let them keep their own culture.

Rarely now do Californians express a confidence in our national culture or a willingness to defend the larger values of Western civilization. The result is that our public schools are either apathetic about, or outright hostile to, the Western paradigm—even as millions from the south risk their lives to enjoy what we so often smugly dismiss. We do not teach immigrant or native-born children that free association, free speech, free inquiry, and the material prosperity that springs from the sanctity of private property and free markets are the essential elements that preserve the dignity of the individual that we enjoy. Our elites do not understand just how rare consensual government is in the history of civilization, and therefore they wrongly think that they can instill confidence by praising the other, less successful, cultures that aliens are escaping from rather than explaining the dynamism and morality of the civilization that they have voted for with their feet.

Our schools, through multiculturalism, cultural relativism, and a therapeutic curriculum, often promote the very tribalism, statism, and group rather than individual interests that our new immigrants are fleeing from. If taken to heart, such ideas lead our new arrivals to abject failure in California. Moreover, if we were to entertain attitudes toward women that exist in Mexico, emulate its approach to religious diversity, copy the Mexican constitution, court system, schools, universities, tax code, bureaucracy, energy industry, or power grid, millions of Mexicans quite simply would stay put where they are. Indeed, even the most pro-Mexico Mexican native in America never chooses to forgo the Western emergency room for the herbalist and exorcist in times of acute sickness or gunshot trauma. He does not complain that the American middle class is too large, the water too clean, the gasoline not adulterated, the food too abundant and noninfectious. Nor does he lament the absence of uniformed machine-gun-carrying soldiers on his block. Illegal aliens clamor for reduced tuition for their offspring at supposedly biased UC campuses, not native fellowships for them to enroll in Mexican universities. I often suggest to teachers who tell aliens that our culture is racist, exploitative, and sexist that they should live in Mexico themselves to fathom why millions are dying to obtain what they so casually dismiss.

The sheer numbers of new immigrants presented a golden opportunity for the demagogue. And sure enough, at times of racial tension, you can see brazen agitators on the street with bullhorns and picket signs. Some are organized by MEChA (Movimiento Estudiantil Chicano de Aztlán)—one of whose mottoes once was: "For our race, everything; for those outside our race, nothing." Sometimes the provocateur shows up at a local school, after a Chicano gang has kicked to near death a (Mexican-American) school guard and consequently been expelled.

With megaphone—and with the six o'clock news cameras rolling—he screams about "targeting La Raza" and "keeping the brown down." "There is only one gang who murders in Fresno," he announces at his poorly attended press conference, "and they wear police blue."

The brawling provocateur is as old as America itself, and today's California demagogue harks back to the urban ward bosses of old. More than a century too late, he shares their nineteenth-century vision of enormous ethnic blocs, entirely unassimilated, with tough ramrods like himself at their head—but with the added advantage that his Mexican immigrant constituency in the new age of multiculturalism might be permanent rather than destined to assimilate. His chief fear, I think, is that immigration may slow down; that millions may read and write excellent English; that his brother or sister—or he himself—may marry the white or Asian other; that a Mexican middle class might emerge in private enterprise outside of government entitlement and civil service; that the Mexican propensity for duty, family, and self-sacrifice might yet make him obsolete; that we all might integrate and forget about race; that he will not be needed and thus not have to be bargained off.

Other opportunists—for some reason, more often Hispanic than native American—are the products of Chicano, Latino, La Raza, or Hispanic studies programs at universities. (Could we ever tolerate any other university program or national organization dubbed "The Race"?) They are the well-meaning Latino elites who have suddenly reverted from Alex to Alejandro and have never met an "r" they won't trill. These self-appointed leaders are professed tribalists—who do not wish to live within the tribe. They may make speeches and films about gang violence and teen pregnancy, but they never really tell us why these endemic problems came into being and how they can be prevented. They leave cause and effect unspoken, allege racism and victimization, not a failure to learn English and accept a common culture—and then they go home in SUVs to upscale suburban homes well apart from the unassimilated barrios they claim to represent.

This state, like the country at large, was a raw experiment, a multiracial society united by a common language, culture, and law. But that subjugation of race to culture is forever a fragile creation, not a natural entity. Each day it can erode. A single fool can undo the work of decades and so allow small people to feel one with those of like tongue and skin color, not united by shared ideals and values. Thus each time a university president, a politician on the make, or a would-be muckraking journalist chooses the easy path of separatism, he, like the white chauvinists of the past, does his own little part in turning us into Rwanda or Kosovo. The wrong message at the top eventually filters down to the newly arrived and helps determine whether they succeed or fail in the no-nonsense arena of America.

How did the old assimilationist model work? Brutally and effectively. In our grammar schools during the 1950s and 1960s, no Spanish was to be spoken on the playground—officially, at least. Groups of four and larger were not allowed to congregate at recess. When we were caught fighting, nontraditional kicking instead of the accepted punching earned four, rather than two, spankings. A rather tough Americanism in class was rammed down our throats—biographies of Teddy Roosevelt, stories about Lou Gehrig, a repertory of a dozen or so patriotic songs, recitations from Longfellow, and demonstrations of how to fold the flag. "Manners" and "civics" were taught each week, with weird lessons about not appearing "loud" in public or wearing glittery or showy clothes, and especially not staring down strangers or giving people the "hard look" with the intent of "being unpleasant." Our teachers were at times insufferable in their condescension as they disclosed the formula for "making it in America"— but make it in America the vast majority of these immigrants did.

Apparently these rather unsophisticated teachers thought that learning to master English and acquire the rudiments of math, American literature, and national culture were more valuable to the immigrant than were racial studies, Chicano dance, and other popular courses now *au courant* and designed to instill ethnic pride. As I can best fathom it some forty years later, their egalitarian aim was to create a mass of students who would reach high school with equal chances of success. And so they gave us detention for silly things like mispronouncing names and other felonies like chewing gum, handing our papers in without our names written on the upper-right-hand corner, and wearing Frisco baggy pants.

Most of the kids I saw each day then—just as most of the adults I see daily now around the same farm—were from Mexico. Skin color and national origin were quite out in the open. We five Anglos in our class of forty at our rural elementary school were labeled "white boys" and "gringos"; in turn, we knew the majority as "Mexicans," their parents more respectfully as "Mexican Americans." Most fights, however, were not racial. We in the white minority fought beside and against Mexican Americans; the great dividing line of most rumbles was whether you were born in Selma or Fresno. We had our fringe racists, of course: Mr. Martinez, the fourth-grade teacher, told me in 1963 that "whitey was through in California," even as Mrs. Wilson, a Texas native, complimented those in the art class who were "lighter than most from Mexico." There was nothing of the contemporary multicultural model— no bilingual aides, written and spoken communication with parents in Spanish, textbooks highlighting the Aztecs and the theft of northern Mexico, or federally funded counselors to remind students that "the borders crossed us, not we the borders." Excused absences for catechism classes at the Catholic church emptied our classrooms, giving us five Anglo Protestants a much-welcomed three-hour recess. We all suffered fish sticks on Friday, the public school's concession to the vast Catholic majority.

That elementary school is still two miles away, but whereas forty years ago it turned out educated and confident Americans, its graduates who enter high school now have among the lowest literacy levels and most dismal math skills in the state. The lucky ones who go on to college generally end up in the California State University system's remedial classes. Yet just reaching those remedial programs is a great achievement in itself. In 1996 the high school graduation rate of California's Hispanics—both native and foreign-born—was only 61 percent. And of those still in high school by their senior year, only 50 percent of Hispanic students met "basic" standards of twelfth-grade math—compared with 80 percent of whites. A mere 6 percent tested "proficient." That means that, out of every hundred Hispanics who now enter California high schools, forty will drop out. And of the remaining sixty, fewer than four will matriculate prepared for any serious college-level courses in mathematics. Only 7 percent of all Mexican Americans currently hold a B.A. In short, this is a national tragedy.

Yet few of the Mexican-American friends I grew up with speak fluent Spanish anymore, regardless of whether they finished college. Completing eighth grade then provided a far better education than finishing high school does now. All of them are well informed and can read, write, compute, and understand the basic tenets of the culture that they have helped build and maintain—and that they most certainly think is far superior to Mexico's. Their children know only a few words of Spanish—by contrast with the present 65 percent of all Hispanic foreign-born in the United States who now speak only "limited English." Most of my generation have become insurance salesmen, mechanics, contractors, teachers, civil servants, occasionally wealthy businessmen and high-government bureaucrats—in other words, the present-day future of California. There are no Mexican flags on their cars, which more likely sport decals like "Proud Parent of a Lincoln School Honors Student" or "*Semper Fi.*" About half, it seems to me, are not married to Mexican Americans.

Most vote as conservative Democrats, are probably anti-abortion, and perhaps even support the death penalty. Some joined and prospered in the Marines; others run the Lions and Kiwanis. They are sensitive to occasional news of ethnic prejudice yet display little affinity for the La Raza industry. In their daily lives they are more worried about gangs and Mexican crime than white racism; most are ambivalent about having thousands of new illegal aliens arrive into their small towns from central Mexico. A few seem to be conscious of race only when the father is Anglo, the mother Mexican: affirmative action, they believe, takes a dimmer view of a Justin Smith who is half-Mexican than a Justin Martinez. Their loss of indigenous culture is sad, perhaps—but no sadder than my own failure to speak Swedish, put cow-horn helmets on my wall, care much about Leif Eriksson, defend Swedish duplicity in World War II, or buy Volvos and Electrolux vacuums out of ethnic pride.

I often think that if I did not particularly like my Mexican-American students (who make up the majority of my classics classes), and if I wanted them to fail, I would not continue to teach them Latin (much less Greek), English composition, or Western history and culture. Nor would I insist on essays free of grammatical error or demand oral reports that employ classical rhetorical tropes.

No, if I did not like them or did not wish to live among thousands of illegal and legal immigrants and wish them married into my family, I would keep them distant by teaching them therapy, letting them speak poor English— or no English at all—and insisting on the superiority of the Mexican culture that they or their parents had fled. If I did not like my students and wished them to remain in the fields—or when they were employed in the office to be snickered at behind closed doors by their white benefactors—I would move from the west side of Selma to an exclusive white suburb in north Fresno, and then as penance teach them during the day about the glory of the Aztecs, the need for government entitlement, and the idea that grammar is but a "construct." I would insist that white racism and capitalist brutality alone explain Mexican-American crime rates, and I would explain why they need someone like me to champion their cause to the wealthy and educated. If I really wished to be distant from my students, I would insist that they attend our university's separate Hispanic graduation assemblies to remind them that they are intrinsically different from, rather than inherently equal to, me. I would be more like the sensitive teachers who teach today than the insensitive ones who once taught me.

So I have made my choice on the great question that California must decide: whether we will remain multiracial or become America's first truly multicultural state. For our future, will we all return to an imperfect, insensitive, but honest assimilationist past that nevertheless worked, or stay with the utopian and deceitful multiculturalist present that is clearly failing? Unchecked illegal immigration and multiculturalism are a lethal mix. California—if it is to stay as California—might have coped with one or even the other, but surely not both at once.

2

STEVEN MALANGA

How Unskilled Immigrants Hurt Our Economy

The day after Librado Velasquez arrived on Staten Island after a long, surreptitious journey from his Chiapas, Mexico, home, he headed out to a street corner to wait with other illegal immigrants looking for work. Velasquez, who had supported his wife, seven kids, and his in-laws as a *campesino*, or peasant farmer, until a 1998 hurricane devastated his farm, eventually got work, off the books, loading trucks at a small New Jersey factory, which hired illegals for jobs that required few special skills. The arrangement suited both, until a work injury sent Velasquez to the local emergency room, where federal law required that he be treated, though he could not afford to pay for his care. After five operations he is now permanently disabled and remains in the United States to pursue compensation claims.

"I do not have the use of my leg without walking with a cane, and I do not have strength in my arm in order to lift things," Velasquez said through an interpreter at New York City Council hearings. "I have no other way to live except if I receive some other type of compensation. I need help, and I thought maybe my son could come and work here and support me here in the United States."

Velasquez's story illustrates some of the fault lines in the nation's current, highly charged debate on immigration. Since the mid-1960s America has welcomed nearly thirty million legal immigrants and received perhaps another fifteen million illegals, numbers unprecedented in our history. These immigrants have picked our fruit, cleaned our homes, cut our grass, worked in our factories, and washed our cars. But they have also crowded into our hospital emergency rooms, schools, and government-subsidized aid programs, sparking a fierce debate about their contributions to our society and the costs they impose on it.

Advocates of open immigration argue that welcoming the Librado Velasquezes of the world is essential for our American economy: our businesses need workers like him because we have a shortage of people willing to do low-wage work. Moreover, the free movement of labor in a global economy pays off for the United States because immigrants bring skills and capital that expand our economy and offset immigration's costs. Like tax cuts, supporters argue, immigration pays for itself.

But the tale of Librado Velasquez helps show why supporters are wrong about today's immigration, as many Americans sense and as so much research has demonstrated. America does not have a vast labor shortage that requires waves of low-wage immigrants to alleviate; in fact, unemployment among native-born unskilled workers is high—consistently about double the nation's overall unemployment rate. Moreover, many of the unskilled, uneducated workers now journeying here labor, like Velasquez, in shrinking industries, where they force out native workers, and many others work in industries where the availability of cheap workers has led businesses to suspend investment in new technologies that would make them less labor-intensive.

Yet while these workers add little to our economy, they come at great cost, because they are not economic abstractions but human beings, with their own culture and ideas—often at odds with our own. Increasing numbers of them arrive with little education and none of the skills necessary to succeed in a modern economy. Many may wind up stuck on our lowest economic rungs, where they will rely on something that immigrants of other generations didn't have: a vast U.S. welfare and social-services apparatus that has enormously amplified the cost of immigration. Just as welfare reform and other policies are helping to shrink America's underclass by weaning people off such social programs, we are importing a new, foreign-born underclass. As famed free-market economist Milton Friedman put it: "It's just obvious that you can't have free immigration and a welfare state."

Immigration can only pay off again for America if we reshape our policy, organizing it around what's good for the economy by welcoming workers we truly need and excluding those who, because they have so little to offer, are likely to cost us more than they contribute, and who will struggle for years to find their place here.

Hampering today's immigration debate are our misconceptions about the so-called first great migration some 100 years ago, with which today's immigration is often compared. We envision that first great migration as a time when multitudes of Emma Lazarus's "tired," "poor," and "wretched refuse" of Europe's shores made their way from destitution to American opportunity. Subsequent studies of American immigration with titles like *The Uprooted* convey the same impression of the dispossessed and displaced swarming here to find a new life. If America could assimilate 24 million mostly desperate immigrants from that great migration—people one unsympathetic economist at the turn of the twentieth century described as "the unlucky, the thriftless, the worthless"—surely, so the story goes, today's much bigger and richer country can absorb the millions of Librado Velasquezes now venturing here.

But that argument distorts the realities of the first great migration. Although fleeing persecution or economic stagnation in their homelands, that era's immigrants—Jewish tailors and seamstresses who helped create New York's garment industry, Italian stonemasons and bricklayers who helped build some of our greatest buildings, German merchants, shopkeepers, and artisans—all brought important skills with them that fit easily into the

American economy. Those waves of immigrants—many of them urban dwellers who crossed a continent and an ocean to get here—helped supercharge the workforce at a time when the country was going through a transformative economic expansion that craved new workers, especially in its cities. A 1998 National Research Council report noted "that the newly arriving immigrant nonagricultural work force . . . was (slightly) more skilled than the resident American labor force": 27 percent of them were skilled laborers, compared with only 17 percent of that era's native-born workforce.

Many of these immigrants quickly found a place in our economy, participating in the workforce at a higher rate even than the native population. Their success at finding work sent many of them quickly up the economic ladder: those who stayed in America for at least fifteen years, for instance, were just as likely to own their own business as native-born workers of the same age, one study found. Another study found that their American-born children were just as likely to be accountants, engineers, or lawyers as Americans whose families had been here for generations.

What the newcomers of the great migration did not find here was a vast social-services and welfare state. They had to rely on their own resources or those of friends, relatives, or private, often ethnic, charities if things did not go well. That's why about 70 percent of those who came were men in their prime. It's also why many of them left when the economy sputtered several times during the period. For though one often hears that restrictive anti-immigration legislation starting with the Emergency Quota Act of 1921 ended the first great migration, what really killed it was the crash of the American economy. Even with the 1920s quotas, America welcomed some 4.1 million immigrants, but in the depression of the 1930s the number of foreign immigrants tumbled far below quota levels, to 500,000. With America's streets no longer paved with gold, and without access to New Deal programs for native-born Americans, immigrants not only stopped coming but some 60 percent of those already here left in a great remigration home, according to a 1998 National Academy of Sciences study.

Today's immigration has turned out so differently in part because it emerged out of the 1960s civil rights and Great Society mentality. In 1965 a new immigration act eliminated the old system of national quotas, which critics saw as racist because it greatly favored European nations. Lawmakers created a set of broader immigration quotas for each hemisphere, and they added a new visa preference category for family members to join their relatives here. Senate immigration subcommittee chairman Edward Kennedy reassured the country that, "contrary to the charges in some quarters, [the bill] will not inundate America with immigrants," and "it will not cause American workers to lose their jobs."

But in fact the law had an immediate, dramatic effect, increasing immigration by 60 percent in its first ten years. Sojourners from poorer countries around the rest of the world arrived in ever-greater numbers, so that whereas half of immigrants in the 1950s had originated from Europe, 75 percent by the 1970s were from Asia and Latin America. And as the influx of immigrants grew, the special-preferences rule for family unification intensified it further, as the pool of eligible family members around the world also increased. Legal immigration to the United States soared from 2.5 million in the 1950s to 4.5 million in the 1970s, to 7.3 million in the 1980s, to about 10 million in the 1990s.

As the floodgates of legal immigration opened, the widening economic gap between the United States and many of its neighbors also pushed illegal immigration to levels that America had never seen. In particular, when Mexico's move to a more centralized, state-run economy in the 1970s produced hyperinflation, the disparity between its stagnant economy and U.S. prosperity yawned wide. Mexico's per capita gross domestic product, 37 percent of the United States' in the early 1980s, was only 27 percent of it by the end of the decade—and is now just 25 percent of it. With Mexican farmworkers able to earn seven to ten times as much in the United States as at home, by the 1980s illegals were pouring across the border at the rate of about 225,000 a year, and U.S. sentiment rose for slowing the flow.

But an unusual coalition of business groups, unions, civil rights activists, and church leaders thwarted the call for restrictions with passage of the inaptly named 1986 Immigration Reform and Control Act, which legalized some 2.7 million unauthorized aliens already here, supposedly in exchange for tougher penalties and controls against employers who hired illegals. The law proved no deterrent, however, because supporters, in subsequent legislation and court cases argued on civil rights grounds, weakened the employer sanctions. Meanwhile more illegals flooded here in the hope of future amnesties from

Congress, while the newly legalized sneaked their wives and children into the country rather than have them wait for family-preference visas. The flow of illegals into the country rose to between 300,000 and 500,000 per year in the 1990s, so that a decade after the legislation that had supposedly solved the undocumented alien problem by reclassifying them as legal, the number of illegals living in the United States was back up to about 5 million, while today it's estimated at 11 million.

The flood of immigrants, both legal and illegal, from countries with poor, ill-educated populations, has yielded a mismatch between today's immigrants and the American economy and has left many workers poorly positioned to succeed for the long term. Unlike the immigrants of a hundred years ago, whose skills reflected or surpassed those of the native workforce at the time, many of today's arrivals, particularly the more than half who now come from Central and South America, are farmworkers in their home countries who come here with little education or even basic training in blue-collar occupations like carpentry or machinery. (A century ago, farmworkers made up 35 percent of the U.S. labor force, compared with the less than 2 percent who produce a surplus of food today.) Nearly two-thirds of Mexican immigrants, for instance, are high school dropouts, and most wind up doing either unskilled factory work or small-scale construction projects, or they work in service industries, where they compete for entry-level jobs against one another, against the adult children of other immigrants, and against native-born high school dropouts. Of the fifteen industries employing the greatest percentage of foreign-born workers, half are low-wage service industries, including gardening, domestic household work, car washes, shoe repair, and janitorial work. To take one stark example: whereas a hundred years ago immigrants were half as likely as native-born workers to be employed in household service, today immigrants account for 27 percent of all domestic workers in the United States.

Although open-borders advocates say that these workers are simply taking jobs Americans don't want, studies show that the immigrants drive down wages of native-born workers and squeeze them out of certain industries. Harvard economists George Borjas and Lawrence Katz, for instance, estimate that low-wage immigration cuts the wages for the average native-born high school dropout by some 8 percent, or more than $1,200 a year. Other economists find that the new workers also push down wages significantly for immigrants already here and for native-born Hispanics.

Consequently, as the waves of immigration continue, the sheer number of those competing for low-skilled service jobs makes economic progress difficult. A study of the impact of immigration on New York City's restaurant business, for instance, found that 60 percent of immigrant workers do not receive regular raises while 70 percent had never been promoted. One Mexican dishwasher aptly captured the downward pressure that all these arriving workers put on wages by telling the study's authors about his frustrating search for a 50-cent raise after working for $6.50 an hour: "I visited a few restaurants asking for $7 an hour, but they only offered me $5.50 or $6," he said. "I had to beg [for a job]."

Similarly, immigration is also pushing some native-born workers out of jobs, as Kenyon College economists showed in the California nail-salon workforce. Over a 16-year period starting in the late 1980s, some 35,600 mostly Vietnamese immigrant women flooded into the industry, a mass migration that equaled the total number of jobs in the industry before the immigrants arrived. Although the new workers created a labor surplus that led to lower prices, new services, and somewhat more demand, the economists estimate that as a result, 10,000 native-born workers either left the industry or never bothered entering it.

In many American industries, waves of low-wage workers have also retarded investments that might lead to modernization and efficiency. Farming, which employs a million immigrant laborers in California alone, is the prime case in point. Faced with a labor shortage in the early 1960s, when President Kennedy ended a 22-year-old guest-worker program that allowed 45,000 Mexican farmhands to cross over the border and harvest 2.2 million tons of California tomatoes for processed foods, farmers complained but swiftly automated, adopting a mechanical tomato-picking technology created more than a decade earlier. Today just 5,000 better-paid workers—one-ninth the original workforce—harvest 12 million tons of tomatoes using the machines.

The savings prompted by low-wage migrants may even be minimal in crops not easily mechanized. Agricultural economists Wallace Huffman and Alan McCunn of Iowa State University have estimated that without illegal workers, the retail cost of fresh produce would increase only about 3 percent in the summer-fall season and less than 2 percent in the winter-spring season, because labor represents only a tiny percent of the retail price of produce, and because without migrant workers America would probably import more foreign fruits and vegetables. "The question is whether we want to import more produce from abroad, or more workers from abroad to pick our produce," Huffman remarks.

For American farmers, the answer has been to keep importing workers—which has now made the farmers more vulnerable to foreign competition, since even minimum-wage immigrant workers can't compete with produce picked on farms in China, Chile, or Turkey and shipped here cheaply. A flood of low-priced Turkish raisins several years ago produced a glut in the United States that sharply drove down prices and knocked some farms out of business, shrinking total acreage in California devoted to the crop by one-fifth, or some fifty thousand acres. The farms that survived are now moving to mechanize swiftly, realizing that no amount of cheap immigrant labor will make them competitive.

As foreign competition and mechanization shrink manufacturing and farmworker jobs, low-skilled immigrants are likely to wind up further on the margins of our economy, where many already operate. For example, although only about 12 percent of construction workers are foreign-born, 100,000 to 300,000 illegal immigrants have carved a place for themselves as temporary workers on the fringes of the industry. In urban areas like New York and Los Angeles, these mostly male illegal immigrants gather on street corners, in empty lots, or in Home Depot parking lots to sell their labor by the hour or the day, for $7 to $11 an hour.

That's far below what full-time construction workers earn, and for good reason. Unlike the previous generations of immigrants who built America's railroads or great infrastructure projects like New York's bridges and tunnels, these day laborers mostly do home-improvement projects. A New York study, for instance, found that four in ten employers who hire day laborers are private homeowners or renters wanting help with cleanup chores, moving, or landscaping. Another 56 percent were contractors, mostly small, nonunion shops, some owned by immigrants themselves, doing short-term, mostly residential work. The day laborer's market, in other words, has turned out to be a boon for homeowners and small contractors offering their residential clients a rock-bottom price, but a big chunk of the savings comes because low-wage immigration has produced such a labor surplus that many of these workers are willing to take jobs without benefits and with salaries far below industry norms.

Because so much of our legal and illegal immigrant labor is concentrated in such fringe, low-wage employment, its overall impact on our economy is extremely small. A 1997 National Academy of Sciences study estimated that immigration's net benefit to the American economy raises the average income of the native-born by only some $10 billion a year—about $120 per household. And that meager contribution is not the result of immigrants helping to build our essential industries or making us more competitive globally but instead merely delivering our pizzas and cutting our grass. Estimates by pro-immigration forces that foreign workers contribute much more to the economy, boosting annual gross domestic product by hundreds of billions of dollars, generally just tally what immigrants earn here while ignoring the offsetting effect they have on the wages of native-born workers.

If the benefits of the current generation of migrants are small, the costs are large and growing because of America's vast range of social programs and the wide advocacy network that strives to hook low-earning legal and illegal immigrants into these programs. A 1998 National Academy of Sciences study found that more than 30 percent of California's foreign-born were on Medicaid—including 37 percent of all Hispanic households—compared with 14 percent of native-born households. The foreign-born were more than twice as likely as the native-born to be on welfare, and their children were nearly five times as likely to be in means-tested government lunch programs. Native-born households pay for much of this, the study found, because they earn more and pay higher taxes—and are more likely to comply with tax laws. Recent immigrants, by contrast, have much lower levels of income and tax compliance (another study estimated that only 56 percent of illegals in California have taxes withheld from their earnings). The study's conclusion: immigrant families cost each native-born household in California an additional $1,200 a year in taxes.

Immigration's bottom line has shifted so sharply that in a high-immigration state like California, native-born residents are paying up to ten times more in state and local taxes than immigrants generate in economic benefits.

Moreover, the cost is only likely to grow as the foreign-born population—which has already mushroomed from about 9 percent of the U.S. population when the NAS studies were done in the late 1990s to about 12 percent today—keeps growing. And citizens in more and more places will feel the bite as immigrants move beyond their traditional settling places. From 1990 to 2005, the number of states in which immigrants make up at least 5 percent of the population nearly doubled, from seventeen to twenty-nine, with states like Arkansas, South Dakota, South Carolina, and Georgia seeing the most growth. This sharp turnaround since the 1970s, when immigrants were less likely to be using the social programs of the Great Society than the native-born population, says Harvard economist Borjas, suggests that welfare and other social programs are a magnet drawing certain types of immigrants—nonworking women, children, and the elderly—and keeping them here when they run into difficulty.

Not only have the formal and informal networks helping immigrants tap into our social spending grown, but they also get plenty of assistance from advocacy groups financed by tax dollars, working to ensure that immigrants get their share of social spending. Thus the Newark-based New Jersey Immigration Policy Network receives several hundred thousand government dollars annually to help doctors and hospitals increase immigrant enrollment in Jersey's subsidized health-care programs. Casa Maryland, operating in the greater Washington area, gets funding from nearly twenty federal, state, and local government agencies to run programs that "empower" immigrants to demand benefits and care from government and to "refer clients to government and private social service programs for which they and their families may be eligible."

·Pols around the country, intent on currying favor with ethnic voting blocs by appearing immigrant-friendly, have jumped on the benefits-for-immigrants bandwagon, endorsing "don't ask, don't tell" policies toward immigrants who register for benefits, giving tax dollars to centers that find immigrants work and aid illegals, and enacting legislation prohibiting local authorities from cooperating with federal immigration officials. In New York, for instance, Mayor Michael Bloomberg has ordered city agencies to ignore an immigrant's status in providing services. "This policy's critical to encourage immigrant day laborers to access . . . children's health insurance, a full range of preventive primary and acute medical care, domestic violence counseling, emergency shelters, police protection, consumer fraud protections, and protection against discrimination through the Human Rights Commission," the city's Immigrant Affairs Commissioner, Guillermo Linares, explains.

Almost certainly, immigrants' participation in our social welfare programs will increase over time, because so many are destined to struggle in our workforce. Despite our cherished view of immigrants as rapidly climbing the economic ladder, more and more of the new arrivals and their children face a lifetime of economic disadvantage, because they arrive here with low levels of education and with few work skills—shortcomings not easily overcome. Mexican immigrants, who are up to six times more likely to be high school dropouts than native-born Americans, not only earn substantially less than the native-born median but the wage gap persists for decades after they've arrived. A study of the 2000 census data, for instance, shows that Mexican immigrants between twenty-five and thirty-four who entered the United States in the late 1970s were earning 40 to 50 percent less than similarly aged native-born Americans in 1980, but twenty years later they had fallen even further behind their native-born counterparts. Today's Mexican immigrants between twenty-five and thirty-four have an even larger wage gap relative to the native-born population. Adjusting for other socio-economic factors, Harvard's Borjas and Katz estimate that virtually this entire wage gap is attributable to low levels of education.

Meanwhile, because their parents start off so far behind, the American-born children of Mexican immigrants also make slow progress. First-generation adult Americans of Mexican descent studied in the 2000 census, for instance, earned 14 percent less than native-born Americans. By contrast, first-generation Portuguese Americans earned slightly more than the average native-born worker—a reminder of how quickly immigrants once succeeded in America and how some still do. But Mexico increasingly dominates our immigration flows, accounting for 43 percent of the growth of our foreign-born population in the 1990s.

One reason some ethnic groups make up so little ground concerns the transmission of what economists call "ethnic capital," or what we might call the influence of culture. More than previous generations, immigrants today tend to live concentrated in ethnic enclaves, and their children find their role models among their own group. Thus the children of today's Mexican immigrants are likely to live in a neighborhood where about 60 percent of men dropped out of high school and now do low-wage work, and where less than half the population speak English fluently—which might explain why high school dropout rates among Americans of Mexican ancestry are two and a half times higher than dropout rates for all other native-born Americans, and why first-generation Mexican Americans do not move up the economic ladder nearly as quickly as the children of other immigrant groups.

In sharp contrast is the cultural capital transmitted by Asian immigrants to children growing up in predominantly Asian-American neighborhoods. More than 75 percent of Chinese immigrants and 98 percent of South Asian immigrants to the United States speak English fluently, while a mid-1990s study of immigrant households in California found that 37 percent of Asian immigrants were college graduates, compared with only 3.4 percent of Mexican immigrants. Thus even an Asian-American child whose parents are high school dropouts is more likely to grow up in an environment that encourages him to stay in school and learn to speak English well, attributes that will serve him well in the job market. Not surprisingly, several studies have shown that Asian immigrants and their children earn substantially more than Mexican immigrants and their children.

Given these realities, several of the major immigration reforms now under consideration simply don't make economic sense—especially the guest-worker program favored by President Bush and the U.S. Senate. Careful economic research tells us that there is no significant shortfall of workers in essential American industries, desperately needing supplement from a massive guest-worker program. Those few industries now relying on cheap labor must focus more quickly on mechanization where possible. Meanwhile the cost of paying legal workers already here a bit more to entice them to do such low-wage work as is needed will have a minimal impact on our economy.

The potential woes of a guest-worker program, moreover, far overshadow any economic benefit, given what we know about the long, troubled history of temporary-worker programs in developed countries. They have never stemmed illegal immigration, and the guest workers inevitably become permanent residents, competing with the native-born and forcing down wages. Our last guest-worker program with Mexico, begun during World War II to boost wartime manpower, grew larger in the postwar era, because employers who liked the cheap labor lobbied hard to keep it. By the mid-1950s the number of guest workers reached seven times the annual limit during the war itself, while illegal immigration doubled as the availability of cheap labor prompted employers to search for ever more of it rather than invest in mechanization or other productivity gains.

The economic and cultural consequences of guest-worker programs have been devastating in Europe, and we risk similar problems. When post–World War II Germany permitted its manufacturers to import workers from Turkey to man the assembly lines, industry's investment in productivity declined relative to such countries as Japan, which lacked ready access to cheap labor. When Germany finally ended the guest-worker program once it became economically unviable, most of the guest workers stayed on, having attained permanent-resident status. Since then, the descendants of these workers have been chronically underemployed and now have a crime rate double that of German youth.

France has suffered similar consequences. In the post–World War II boom, when French unemployment was under 2 percent, the country imported an industrial labor force from its colonies; by the time France's industrial jobs began evaporating in the 1980s, these guest workers and their children numbered in the millions, and most had made little economic progress. They now inhabit the vast housing projects, or *cités*, that ring Paris— and that have recently been the scene of chronic rioting. Like Germany, France thought it was importing a labor force, but it wound up introducing a new underclass.

"Importing labor is far more complicated than importing other factors of production, such as commodities," write University of California at Davis professor Philip Martin, an expert on guest-worker programs, and Michael Teitelbaum, a former member of the U.S. Commission on Immigration Reform. "Migration involves human beings, with their own beliefs, politics, cultures, languages, loves, hates, histories, and families."

If low-wage immigration doesn't pay off for the United States, legalizing illegals already here makes as little sense as importing new rounds of guest workers. The Senate and President Bush, however, aim to start two-thirds of the eleven million undocumented aliens already in the country on a path to legalization, on the grounds that only thus can America assimilate them, and only through assimilation can they hope for economic success in the United States. But such arguments ignore the already poor economic performance of increasingly large segments of the *legal* immigrant population in the United States. Merely granting illegal aliens legal status won't suddenly catapult them up our mobility ladder, because it won't give them the skills and education to compete.

At the same time legalization will only spur new problems, as our experience with the 1986 immigration act should remind us. At the time, then-congressman Charles Schumer, who worked on the legislation, acknowledged that it was "a riverboat gamble," with no certainty that it would slow down the waves of illegals. Now, of course, we know that the legislation had the opposite effect, creating the bigger problem we now have (which hasn't stopped Senator Schumer from supporting the current legalization proposals). The legislation also swamped the Immigration and Naturalization Service with masses of fraudulent, black-market documents, so that it eventually rubber-stamped tens of thousands of dubious applications.

If we do not legalize them, what can we do with eleven million illegals? Ship them back home? Their presence here is a fait accompli, the argument goes, and only legalization can bring them aboveground, where they can assimilate. But that argument assumes that we have only two choices: to decriminalize or to deport. But what happened after the first great migration suggests a third way: to end the economic incentives that keep them here. We could prompt a great remigration home if, first off, state and local governments in jurisdictions like New York and

California would stop using their vast resources to aid illegal immigrants. Second, the federal government can take the tougher approach that it failed to take after the 1986 act. It can require employers to verify Social Security numbers and immigration status before hiring, so that we bar illegals from many jobs. It can deport those caught here. And it can refuse to give those who remain the same benefits as U.S. citizens. Such tough measures do work: as a recent Center for Immigration Studies report points out, when the federal government began deporting illegal Muslims after 9/11, many more illegals who knew they were likely to face more scrutiny voluntarily returned home.

If America is ever to make immigration work for our economy again, it must reject policies shaped by advocacy groups trying to turn immigration into the next civil rights cause, or by a tiny minority of businesses seeking cheap labor subsidized by the taxpayers. Instead we must look to other developed nations that have focused on luring workers who have skills that are in demand and who have the best chance of assimilating. Australia, for instance, gives preferences to workers grouped into four skilled categories: managers, professionals, associates of professionals, and skilled laborers. Using a straightforward "points calculator" to determine who gets in, Australia favors immigrants between the ages of eighteen and forty-five who speak English, have a post–high school degree or training in a trade, and have at least six months' work experience as everything from laboratory technicians to architects and surveyors to information-technology workers. Such an immigration policy goes far beyond America's employment-based immigration categories, like the

H1-B visas, which account for about 10 percent of our legal immigration and essentially serve the needs of a few Silicon Valley industries.

Immigration reform must also tackle our family-preference visa program, which today accounts for two-thirds of all legal immigration and has helped create a forty-year waiting list. Lawmakers should narrow the family-preference visa program to spouses and minor children of U.S. citizens and should exclude adult siblings and parents.

America benefits even today from many of its immigrants, from the Asian entrepreneurs who have helped revive inner-city Los Angeles business districts to Haitians and Jamaicans who have stabilized neighborhoods in Queens and Brooklyn, to Indian programmers who have spurred so much innovation in places like Silicon Valley and Boston's Route 128. But increasingly over the last twenty-five years, such immigration has become the exception. It needs once again to become the rule.

3

HEATHER MAC DONALD

Seeing Today's
Immigrants Straight

The immigration debate has divided the conservative
movement, with each side accusing the other of betraying
core conservative principles. Amnesty proponents argue
that America's best traditions require legalizing the estimated eleven million illegal aliens already here and opening the door wide to would-be migrants the world over.
Illegal immigration, these conservative advocates say, is
the inevitable and blameless consequence of misguided
laws that foolishly—and vainly—seek to prevent willing
workers and labor-hungry employers from finding each
other. Hispanics—the vast majority of aliens and the real
center of the immigration debate—bring much-needed
family values and a work ethic to the American polity;

refusing to grant them legal status would destroy Republican hopes for a large new voting bloc. Since popular opposition to large-scale Hispanic immigration stems from economic ignorance and nativist fear, policymakers should protect America from its own worst impulses and ignore the anti-immigration revolt.

Conservative opponents of amnesty and liberalized immigration respond that the rule of law is at stake. Rewarding large-scale lawbreaking with legal status and financial benefits will spark further violations. The mass amnesty protests of the spring were part of a growing international movement challenging national sovereignty. Conservative respect for facts should encourage skepticism toward claims of superior Hispanic values. And the conservative preference for local decision-making cautions against dismissing the popular backlash against illegal immigration; it is just possible that people closest to the problem know something that Beltway insiders do not.

Vexing the debate further, the popular revolt is not just against illegal immigration but against high levels of unskilled Mexican immigration per se. As political scientist Peter Skerry observes, the public dislikes the effect on local communities of large numbers of poor Mexicans and their progeny, legal or not. Some of the effects, such as crime, worsen dramatically from the first to the second generation of Mexicans, who not only are legal but are American citizens.

Since criticizing illegal immigration often draws charges of racism, few relish going further and challenging the wisdom of our current immigration flows, legal or not. Yet unless we accurately diagnose the immigration problem, any legislative fix that merely converts the current illegal flow to a legal one will fail both as policy and as politics. Herewith—in an effort to sharpen the internal debate—are the conservative principles that militate against amnesty, for immigration-law enforcement, and for a radical change in immigration priorities.

Principle 1: Respect the law. This year's illegal-alien demonstrators put forward a novel theory of entitlement: because we are here, we have a right to be here. Protesters in Santa Ana, California, shouted: "We are here and we're not going anywhere," reports the *Los Angeles Times*. Anger at the widespread contempt for American law contained in such defiant assertions drives much of the public hostility toward illegal aliens. Conservatives, with their respect for the rule of law and appreciation for its fragility, would ordinarily honor this gut reaction rather than dismissing it as some atavistic tribal impulse. Poverty and other grounds for victim status do not, in the conservative worldview, create a license for lawbreaking.

The rule of law ensures that like cases are treated alike and unlike cases distinguished. But if the immigration protesters have their way, someone who ignored all the procedures for legal entry will achieve the same status and benefits as someone who played by the rules. During the Senate's immigration debates in the spring, amnesty proponents claimed that it was unfair that people who have worked for American employers be forced to "live in the shadows." Left out of the equation was the question of justice to people who have waited for years in their own countries for permission to enter lawfully.

Protecting one form of lawbreaking may require protecting others as well. The city of Maywood in Los Angeles County declared itself a sanctuary zone for illegal aliens this year. Then it got rid of its drunk-driving checkpoints, because they were nabbing too many illegal aliens. Next, this 96 percent Latino city, almost half of whose adult population lacks a ninth-grade education, disbanded its police traffic division entirely, so that illegals wouldn't need to worry about having their cars towed for being unlicensed.

Principle 2: Protect sovereignty. Today's international elites seek to dissolve "discriminatory" distinctions between citizens and noncitizens and to discredit border laws aiming to control the flow of migrants. The spring amnesty demonstrations are a measure of how far such new anti-national-sovereignty ideas have spread. The last large-scale amnesty in 1986 was not preceded by mass demonstrations by illegal aliens but was rather a bargaining chip among American legislators, negotiated in exchange for employer sanctions and a national worker-verification card. Predictably, the card never materialized, and the sanctions were never enforced; only the amnesty lived on.

By contrast, this year's protesters spoke the language of the anti-sovereignty intelligentsia. This increasingly influential discourse was on display at a May conference of Latin American diplomats at the Library of Congress, which spun endless variations on the identical theme: migration is a fundamental human right. As Nicaragua's minister of foreign affairs, Norman Caldera Cardenal, put it: "It is the responsibility of all nations to respect the dignity, integrity, and rights of all migrants." (The delegations dutifully acknowledged the U.S. prerogative to decide its own immigration policy, but these ritual genuflections were insignificant compared with the invocations of migrants' rights.) In less diplomatic language, Mexico's bicameral permanent legislative commission calls American immigration policy "racist, xenophobic, and a profound violation of human rights," reports George Grayson in the *American Conservative*.

Less than a week before the Library of Congress conference, illegal aliens on the streets of Southern California were making the identical demands: "We just want some respect and human rights," a Santa Ana protester told the *Los Angeles Times*. "We're fighting to give [immigrants] equal rights," explained a marcher in Riverside, California, holding a "Legalize, Not Terrorize" sign.

This call for "human rights" is a clever one, for it hides its radical status in a rhetorical safe harbor. What, exactly, are the "human rights" that the United States is denying illegal aliens? They have unfettered access to free medical care, free education, welfare for their children, free representation in court when they commit crimes, every due-process protection during criminal prosecution that the Constitution guarantees citizens and legal immigrants, the shelter of labor laws, and the miracles of modern industrial society like clean water, the control of infectious diseases (including the ones they bring with them), and plumbing. The only putative "right" they lack—and that, of course, is the "human right" to which they and their ambassadors refer—is the right to legal status regardless of illegal entry.

So when the illegal-alien demonstrators and their government representatives demand respect for migrants' "human rights," they are asserting that U.S. immigration laws must fall before a more powerful claim. Despite the nondiscriminatory procedures for entry that Congress established, merely subjecting an illegal alien to an unequal status compared with legal migrants or citizens violates his human rights. Simply creating in his mind the teeniest thought that he may be penalized for his violation of American sovereignty is itself a callous abuse. The director of a Hispanic social-services agency in Georgia complained to the *Atlanta Journal-Constitution* that the federal government's modest immigration arrests in April have "created a mental sickness, where people are depressed. Who wants to be thinking any minute you're going to be arrested?" Mexico's consul general in Austin, Jorge Guajardo, echoed this sense of outrage at the "fear" the immigration arrests had caused: "It doesn't help society or anyone to have these people running scared," he told the *Austin American-Statesman.*

The Bush administration and its conservative supporters have defended American law against international claims to override it. To the applause of conservative pundits, the administration has unsigned the International Criminal Court treaty and withdrawn from the Kyoto global-warming protocol. It refused to wait for UN Security Council approval to start the invasion of Iraq. It has claimed the right to interpret international human rights laws for itself during the war on terror, rather than defer to nonelected bodies like the UN or the International Committee of the Red Cross. Conservative pundits have supported Israel's right to erect a security fence, despite the protestation by the UN International Court of Justice that the fence is illegal. Yet when it comes to immigration law, conservative open-borders advocates and the White House adopt the identical position as the growing anti-sovereignty movement, downplaying the violation of our border law and elevating the "rights" of the illegal migrant to sovereign status.

The illegal-alien rights movement has deployed another powerful contemporary rhetoric: ethnic victimology. As frequent as the demands during the protests to recognize illegals' "human rights" were the demands for "respect." "People have to learn to respect Mexicans, to respect immigrants and the work we do here," an L.A. demonstrator told the *Los Angeles Times*. "Respect for the migrant is fundamental," Costa Rica's minister of foreign affairs told the Library of Congress conference. According to this perspective, immigration policy insults aliens by subjecting them to different statuses according to whether they obeyed the law or not. While the rhetoric of wounded ethnic pride is long in the tooth by now, what is new about today's protests is not only the sense of entitlement with which lawbreakers strike such an attitude, but also that many conservatives back them.

If the Bush administration and its supporters believe that they can reassert the supremacy of American immigration law after yet another amnesty, they are fooling themselves. No one will take the assurance that "this time we mean business" seriously. If the executive branch is not willing to enforce the current law against violators, a new set of laws will not suddenly strengthen its resolve.

The fictions of the proposed guest-worker law are particularly self-deluded. No AWOL guest worker is going to think he faces the slightest risk of deportation, knowing the government won't even penalize people who entered the country illegally from Day One. If the proposed amnesty becomes law, expect illegal immigration to explode, just as it did after the 1986 amnesty, when illegal entry increased fivefold.

Principle 3: Support law enforcement. Come-and-get-it immigration advocates endlessly assert that immigration enforcement can't work. This claim ignores the most important demonstration of conservative principles in the last twenty years.

Elite wisdom for decades held that the police cannot affect crime. The social forces pushing criminals to break the law—poverty, racism, addiction—were too powerful; policing could at best try to solve crimes after they happened. New York's Mayor Giuliani and his first police chief, William Bratton, rejected that fatalism. They empowered the New York Police Department to enforce aggressively laws that had long lain moribund. The targets of the new public-order push complained bitterly that it was unfair to arrest them for marijuana sales and other crimes after years of de facto decriminalization. The NYPD continued its enforcement drive anyway and brought crime down 70 percent in a decade. It turns out that the well-founded fear of getting caught changes behavior.

Conservative open-borders advocates do not explain why policing brings domestic crime down but can have no effect on border crime. Nor can they point to any evidence to support their claim, since immigration laws have never been enforced in the interior of the country. To be sure, border defenses have been fortified over the years, but the drill has been: if you can get past the border patrol, you are home free. The most important action the government could take to end illegal immigration would be to penalize employers that unlawfully hire illegal aliens, but in 2004 it issued fine notices to only three companies. With such a negligible risk of punishment, the law's deterrent effect has been zero. Illegal aliens, for their part, know that in none of their interactions with state services will anyone check their status—including, in most cities, when they are arrested for a crime—nor, if their illegal status is obvious, will anyone report them to the federal government.

Not only is the claim that enforcement doesn't work based on no evidence whatsoever, but in fact what evidence there is runs in the opposite direction. The merest hint of enforcement leads employers and illegal aliens to make different calculations about the advantages of breaking the law. Employers in Gwinnett County, north of Atlanta, have grown reluctant to hire illegals after highly publicized federal raids on an international pallet company in April 2006 and the passage of an omnibus Georgia law that, among other measures, punishes employers for breaking the immigration rules. The state law has not been enforced yet, but already fewer employers are seeking illegal day laborers. A Mexican from Guanajuato told the *Atlanta Journal-Constitution* that he is going back home if the jobs picture doesn't pick up soon; others like him may be making similar plans.

Phoenix teaches the same lesson. Home Depot, on the city's central business artery, for years tolerated the hundreds of illegal Hispanics congregating outside the store and in its parking lot. Neighboring businesses complained bitterly about lost customers and the constant littering, trespassing, and public urination. In May 2006, Home Depot posted signs against trespassing and picking up day laborers, and hired off-duty police officers to enforce the rules. Since then, the day laborers have almost completely disappeared.

Since December 6, 2005, federal agencies have designated a stretch of the Texas border a zero-tolerance zone for border trespassing. Rather than releasing illegal entrants upon capture, the feds jail them for their border crime, then deport them. One border patrol agent told the *Washington Post* that the 51 percent drop in apprehensions since the operation began are "the most dynamic results" he had seen in nineteen years on the force. The *Post* concluded: Operation Streamline II "has shown what it takes to stop the flow of illegal immigrants: aggressive enforcement of the laws on the books."

After 9/11, the Department of Homeland Security deported fifteen hundred illegal Pakistanis. An additional fifteen thousand then left voluntarily, reports Jessica Vaughan of the Center for Immigration Studies. There is no reason to think this enforcement-through-attrition strategy won't work as well for Hispanic illegals. Simply requiring employers to verify the status of their workers would deny jobs to three million illegal workers, which should lead many workers to leave.

Immigration liberalizers wield the threat of mass deportations as the only alternative to amnesty. By now, this argument borders on bad faith, since it has been refuted so many times. The attrition strategy—relying on illegal aliens to leave voluntarily as their access to American benefits diminishes—would work just as effectively, without coercion.

Many open-borders boosters are hawks in the war on terror. But since many of the methods that maintain the border's overall integrity are essential to keeping terrorists out of the country, these boosters should explain why they think we can wink at immigration-border violations and still protect the public against foreign enemies. Either we should give up on keeping immigration lawbreakers *and* terrorists from entering the country, or we should remain vigilant against both, since border security is key to terror protection.

Principle 4: Pay attention to facts on the ground. If someone proposed a program to boost the number of Americans who lack a high school diploma, have children out of wedlock, sell drugs, steal, or use welfare, he'd be deemed mad. Yet liberalized immigration rules would do just that. The illegitimacy rate among Hispanics is high and rising faster than that of other ethnic groups; their dropout rate is the highest in the country; Hispanic children are joining gangs at younger and younger ages. Academic achievement is abysmal.

Conservatives pride themselves on reality-based thinking that rejects utopian theories in favor of facts on the ground. Yet when it comes to immigration, they cling, against all contrary evidence, to the myth of the redeeming power of Hispanic family values, the Hispanic work ethic, and Hispanic virtue. Even more fanciful is the claim that it is immigrants' *children* who constitute the real value to American society. The children of today's Hispanic immigrants, in fact, are in considerable trouble.

Without doubt, many Latinos *are* upwardly mobile. But a significant portion of their children are getting sucked into street life, as a trip to almost any urban high school and some conversations with almost any Hispanic student will verify. In the field, the conservative fact finder would learn that teen pregnancy is pervasive and that Hispanic boys increasingly regard fathering children as the prerequisite to becoming a "playah."

Conservatives have never shrunk from pointing out that dysfunctional behavior creates long-term poverty among inner-city blacks. But when Hispanics engage in the same behavior, they fall silent. From 1990 to 2004, the number of Hispanics in poverty rose 52 percent, accounting for 92 percent of the increase in poor people. The number of poor Hispanic children rose 43 percent, reports *Washington Post* columnist Robert Samuelson. By contrast, the number of poor black children has declined 17 percent since 1990. The influx of dirt-poor Mexicans drives the Hispanic poverty increase, of course, but their behavior once here doesn't help.

Our immigration policy is creating a second underclass, one with the potential to expand indefinitely if current immigration rates merely stay the same, much less treble, as they would under the Hagel-Martinez Senate bill. Given the rapid increase in the Hispanic population, the prevalence of the following socially destructive behavior among Hispanics should be cause for serious concern.

Illegitimacy. Half of all children born to Hispanic Americans in 2002 were illegitimate, twice the rate for American whites and 42 percent higher than the overall American rate. The birthrate for Hispanic teens is higher than that for black teens. In Santa Ana, California, which has the highest proportion of people who speak Spanish at home of any large U.S. city—74 percent—the teen birthrate was twice the national teen average in 2000. This predilection for out-of-wedlock childbearing among Hispanics cannot be blamed solely on corrosive American culture, since the illegitimacy rate for foreign-born Hispanics is 40 percent. The illegitimacy rate in Mexico is 38 percent; in El Salvador, it is 72 percent.

It is hard to reconcile these statistics with the durable myth of superior Hispanic family values. A random walk through Santa Ana encountered ample evidence of Hispanic family breakdown. Livia came illegally from Mexico six years ago and then bore two illegitimate children; she now sells fruit from a pushcart on Main Street. A few blocks away, a twenty-three-year-old illegal unmarried mother from El Salvador is protesting for smaller class sizes (an irony lost on her) outside a Santa Ana school board meeting. She came to the United States at age ten, dropped out of high school, and had her son "really young." He is now on welfare. This unwed mother prides herself on not having had any more children. "So many Latinas are having so many kids," she says disapprovingly. "Kids are having kids."

Even the mainstream media can't help stumbling across the Hispanic illegitimacy epidemic. Reporting on this spring's illegal-alien protests in downtown L.A., the *Los Angeles Times* turned up Guadalupe Aguilera, the mother of five illegitimate children. Aguilera thinks herself self-sacrificing for putting her children only on the WIC federal food program. If she had documents, she said, she could take advantage of a far greater range of welfare benefits. "I lose money that I could give my children," she complained to the *Times*. Increasingly, Hispanic family values mean collecting welfare for out-of-wedlock children.

Academic failure. It would be useful for open-borders optimists to spend some time in the Los Angeles Unified School District, which is 73 percent Hispanic, and where just 40 percent of Hispanic students graduate. (Nationwide, 53 percent of Hispanics graduate from high school, according to the Manhattan Institute's Jay Greene— the lowest rate among all ethnic groups.) Of those Hispanic students who do graduate, just 22 percent have completed the course work necessary for admission to a four-year state college—which means that of all Hispanic students who enter in ninth grade, fewer than 15 percent will graduate ready for college. Immigrant advocates have fiercely opposed in court a long-deferred California high school exit exam, which would require students to answer just over 50 percent of questions testing eighth-grade-level math and ninth-grade-level English. The California Research Bureau predicts that if the exam becomes a reality, Hispanic graduation rates would drop well below 30 percent.

A recent *Los Angeles Times* series on high school dropouts put some faces on the numbers. Eleven male Hispanic friends entered Birmingham High School in Van Nuys together in 2001; only three graduated. Because the boys spent so much time cutting classes—usually hanging out at fast-food restaurants—most failed to log any academic progress and saw no sense in staying enrolled. Drugs, turf rivalries, and fathering children also contributed to their failure to graduate. Birmingham's teachers despair at their students' lack of academic commitment and at their belief that seat time should entitle them to a passing grade. Reports Ronald Fryer in *Education Next*, hostility toward academic achievers is even higher among Hispanics than among blacks.

Schools spend huge sums trying to improve the Hispanic graduation rate, even hiring "outreach consultants" for dropout prevention. One Santa Ana consultant's approach is predictably multicultural. "We need to teach teachers that students need to be proud of where they are coming from," she told me. But, of course, Hispanic school failure derives not from ethnic neglect—the Santa Ana schools glorify the Hispanic heritage to a fault—but from parents who don't demand rigorous academic application and don't stand up to corrosive popular influences. At Santa Ana High School, I spoke with a former student, Julio, who had been expelled as a troublemaker in ninth grade, then returned briefly in the tenth grade but didn't take a single class. "Me and my friends ditched; our parents didn't know." It is the cultural capital that immigrants bring with them that most determines their success; the work ethic of poor Mexicans does not carry over to their children's schooling, and we are all paying the price.

The more-immigrants-the-better proponents counter that early-twentieth-century Italian immigrants were also indifferent to schooling but eventually joined the middle class. But by contrast with the economy of a century ago, today's knowledge-based economy values education above all else. College-educated workers have seen a 22 percent increase in real income since 1980 while high school dropouts lost 3 percent of their wages. High school dropouts will almost certainly remain poor, imposing huge welfare and health-care costs on taxpayers while lowering tax receipts. Native-born Hispanics collected welfare at more than twice the rate of native-born whites in 2005; the foreign-born Hispanic welfare rate was nearly three times that of native-born whites.

Gang culture. In his prime-time May 2006 radio address promoting amnesty, President George Bush invoked a marine, Guadalupe Denogean, as the embodiment of immigrant values. Like Denogean, today's immigrants are willing, said Bush, "to risk everything for the dream of freedom." Many immigrants do share Denogean's patriotic ethic. But for every immigrant soldier, there are as many less admirable counterparts. A selection of Hispanic portraits could just as well have picked out Connie Retana, a thirty-eight-year-old Anaheim, California, resident, who in February egged on her eighteen-year-old son, Martin Delgado, as he and his gang friends raped a twenty-three-year-old for seven hours in retaliation against the young woman's boyfriend. A survey of Hispanic family values might also include the Santa Ana mother who threatened in 2004 to kill her neighbors if they testified against her gangster son in a gun-assault case. Then there's the extended family of criminals in Pomona, California, who raised Valentino Arenas: the eighteen-year-old sought membership in Pomona's 12th Street gang by killing a California highway patrol officer in cold blood in April 2004. Following a sweep in May of the gang, which specializes in large-scale drug trafficking, murder, and extortion, Los Angeles district attorney Steve Cooley excoriated the families across the California Southland who are "aiding and abetting murders in Los Angeles County" by refusing to cooperate with authorities or curtail their children's crimes.

Open-borders conservatives point to the relatively low crime rate among immigrants to deny any connection between high immigration and crime. But unless we can prevent immigrants from having children, a high level of immigration translates to increased levels of crime. Between the foreign-born generation and their American children, the incarceration rate of Mexican Americans jumps more than eightfold, resulting in an incarceration rate that is 3.45 times higher than that of whites, according to an analysis of 2000 census data by the Migration Policy Institute.

California, with one-quarter of the nation's immigrants and its greatest concentration of Mexicans and Central Americans, is the bellwether state for all things relating to unbridled Hispanic immigration, including crime. The Children of Immigrants Longitudinal Study, conducted by sociologists Alejandro Portes of Princeton and Rubén G. Rumbaut of the University of California, Irvine, followed the children of immigrants in San Diego and Miami from 1992 to 2003. A whopping 28 percent of Mexican-American males between the ages of eighteen and twenty-four reported having been arrested since 1995, and 20 percent reported having been incarcerated—a rate twice that of other immigrant groups. Anyone who speaks to Hispanic students in immigrant-saturated schools in

Southern California will invariably hear the estimate that 50 percent of a student's peers have ended up in gangs or other criminal activities.

Gang life—both Hispanic and black—immediately asserted itself last July when the Los Angeles Unified School District opened a model high school to ease overcrowding. Despite amenities that rival those of private schools—a swimming pool, Mac computers, a ballet studio, a rubber running track, and a professional chef's kitchen—it instantly gained the distinction of being one of the most violent campuses in the system. Shots rang out in front of the school on the second day of classes, reports the *Los Angeles Times*, and three days after opening ceremonies, police arrested a student with an AK-47 on the campus perimeter. Brawling students attacked safety officers and tried to grab their guns in December, while cops pepper-sprayed a dean breaking up a gang fight in March. Students sell meth in the classrooms, graffiti covers the stairwells, textbooks, and high-design umbrella-covered picnic tables, and a trip to the bathroom requires an adult safety escort.

Uncertain assimilation. Multicultural cheerleaders argue that assimilation is proceeding apace by pointing to the fact that virtually all third-generation Hispanics can speak English. Even so, linguistic and cultural segregation among Hispanics is increasing. The percentage of Hispanics living in Hispanic enclaves rose from 39 percent in 1990 to 43 percent in 2000, reports Robert Samuelson, and as more and more aliens from Mexico and Central America enter, the size of Spanish-speaking-only areas expands. Livia, the unmarried mother selling fruit on Santa

Ana's Main Street, says that no one she associates with speaks English. A coffee-shop owner down the block observes that it's too easy in Santa Ana not to learn English. "It's all Spanish-speaking here," she says. In California the academic achievement gap between students with little English and English speakers is widening.

Meanwhile taxpayers are footing the bill for interpreters across a host of government functions and for the translation of countless government documents. California spends $82.7 million a year on criminal-court interpreters for those 40 percent of its residents who speak a language other than English at home. At the same time Spanish may be developing into a language of cultural assertion and opposition. A Hispanic resident of El Paso told New York's radio station WNYC in May 2006 that teen workers in fast-food and other retail outlets regularly refuse to answer her in English when she addresses them. At a city council meeting in March 2006 in Maywood, California, the illegal-alien sanctuary, a resident suggested that a council member was using English as a sign of disrespect. All this adds up to a significant, and accelerating, transformation of American culture.

Pro-amnesty forces promote the Ellis Island conceit that illegal immigrants "risk everything for the dream of freedom," as President Bush put it in his May 2006 address. The president's assessment, while flattering, is not particularly accurate. However lousy the Mexican economy, there are few, if any, political freedoms enjoyed by Americans that Mexico denies. It is the Yanqui dollar, not untasted freedom, that brings the vast majority of illegals here. "The dream that most of us hold on to is the Mexican dream," Efrain Jimenez, an official with the Federation of Zacatecan Clubs of Southern California, told me last year. "The Mexican dream is to make enough money to go back and own your own business. Four-fifths of Mexicans here would say that if they had a job in Mexico, they'd go back right away." Most Mexican immigrants do not intend to become Americans; they come wanting to return to their home country but end up staying out of inertia. They naturalize at half the rate of Asians or Europeans. This is not a recipe for assimilation.

Principle 5: Prefer local decision-makers over remote elites. Illegal immigration has prompted a powerful grassroots democratic reaction as people in areas most affected by Hispanic immigration try to regain control of their communities. Cities, counties, and states have passed laws to regulate day-laborer sites, to push employers into compliance with immigration laws, to allow police officers to cooperate with federal immigration agents, to prevent illegal aliens from collecting welfare and from voting, and to tighten driver's-license requirements, among other initiatives.

After appeals from illegal-alien advocacy groups, judges have struck down many of these laws. Ordinarily conservatives would deplore such thwarting of the people's will. When it comes to illegal immigration, however, they side with the elites in robes and on Capitol Hill who dismiss the public as know-nothing rubes. Open-borders conservatives denounce California's Proposition 187 as vehemently as any Hispanic activist, even though the judicially overruled referendum—which denied nonemergency free health care and free public education to illegal aliens—was simply a cry for help from California taxpayers, struggling with the enormous strains that illegal aliens were putting on their state's social welfare systems.

Conservatives have historically trusted local decision-making over distant Washington solutions. The tradition of federalism holds that people closest to a problem are best able to assess and resolve it. Yet the open-borders Right waves away the fervent local lawmaking around illegal immigration as merely an outbreak of xenophobia. Would such conservative legalizers argue that the sixty-three cities and counties that founded the Coalition of Mayors and County Executives for Immigration Reform, a movement trying to alert Washington to the burdens of illegal immigration, have been taken over by racists? Do they really think they themselves see matters more clearly than angry local residents whose local hospital has gone bankrupt under the strain of serving immigrants with no insurance, or than parents who no longer feel welcome in their local schools, or than business owners harmed by the crowds of day laborers on the sidewalk who scare their customers away?

Connecticut's Greenwich Hospital recently treated an illegal Guatemalan with severe drug-resistant TB, after his local hospital in Port Chester, New York, had gone bust from uninsured immigrants. The uncompensated bill for two and a half months of inpatient treatment totaled $200,000, not including the fees for the numerous specialists on the case, which probably added another $100,000 to $150,000. One surgery alone to remove a crippling accretion on his spine—a condition unknown outside the Third World—lasted an entire day. All of the Guatemalan's associates tested positive for TB, and all worked in restaurants, reports his surgeon, Dr. Katrina Firlik, in the *Wall Street Journal*. Such episodes, invisible to conservative elites, make a deep impression on local taxpayers and insurance policyholders.

Arizona and California lawmakers want to free taxpayers from the nearly $1 billion a year burden of detaining illegal criminals—and the even costlier burden of detaining those illegals' children. In Fresno, now 45 percent Hispanic, 20 percent of the county jail inmates are illegal immigrants, as are about one-quarter of emergency-room patients. No wonder Fresno's mayor called in November 2005 for securing the border. The county of Riverside, California, voted in April to start turning in its illegal-alien jail inmates—who make up between 12 and 25 percent of its inmate population—to the Immigration and Customs Enforcement, joining a handful of jail systems now abandoning the long-standing taboo against checking criminals' immigration status. Naturally, immigrant advocates in Southern California have branded the new policy a civil rights violation.

Lived experience fuels these citizen movements for immigration control. If conservatives dismiss them as delusional, the Republican party will pay dearly at the polls. Rather than dismissing the public's anguish over large-scale lawbreaking, conservatives should honor the public's commitment to the sanctity of the legislative will.

The proponents of amnesty have manufactured an artificial crisis. They say it is imperative to legalize the millions of illegals here *now*, so that the illegals can "come out of the shadows." In reality, the minor inconveniences imposed by illegal status are nothing more than what the illegals bargained for. Illegal aliens have no legitimate claim to be legalized *before* the country makes sure that its border control is working. Enforcement must precede a liberalization of immigration rules—which is why "comprehensive" immigration reform (the conservative code word for amnesty and increased levels of immigration) is not the solution to our border crisis but rather a guarantee of continued anarchy. Amnesty and the impossibility of enforcing a complicated new immigration scheme will undermine border control, just as they did in 1986. The first item of business on the conservative agenda should be enforcing the law already on the books.

But the most important value that conservatives can bring to this debate is honesty. Many of the costs imposed by Mexican immigrants are a function of their lack of education, their low incomes, and their own and their children's behavior, not their legal status. Without question, we must balance those costs against the immigrant generation's admirable work ethic. But immigration reform that institutionalizes the present immigration mix—or, worse, increases its volume by three to five times—is certain to expand the Hispanic underclass. There are many educated foreigners patiently waiting for permission to migrate to the United States. The United States can better honor its immigrant heritage by accelerating their entry rather than by continuing to favor the most low-skilled of our neighboring populations.

4

HEATHER MAC DONALD

The Illegal-Alien Crime Wave

Some of the most violent criminals at large today are illegal aliens. Yet in cities where the crime rate of these aliens is highest, the police cannot use the most obvious tool to apprehend them: their immigration status. In Los Angeles, for example, dozens of members of a ruthless Salvadoran prison gang have sneaked back into town after having been deported for such crimes as murder, assault with a deadly weapon, and drug trafficking. Police officers know who they are and know that their mere presence in the country is a felony. Yet should a cop arrest an illegal gangbanger for felonious reentry, it is he who will be treated as a criminal, for violating the LAPD's rule against enforcing immigration law.

The LAPD's ban on immigration enforcement mirrors bans in immigrant-saturated cities around the country, from New York and Chicago to San Diego, Austin, and Houston. These "sanctuary policies" generally prohibit city employees, including the cops, from reporting immigration violations to federal authorities.

Such laws testify to the sheer political power of immigrant lobbies, a power so irresistible that police officials shrink from even mentioning the illegal-alien crime wave. "We can't even talk about it," says a frustrated LAPD captain. "People are afraid of a backlash from Hispanics." Another LAPD commander in a predominantly Hispanic, gang-infested district sighs: "I would get a firestorm of criticism if I talked about [enforcing the immigration law against illegals]." Neither captain would speak for attribution.

But however pernicious in themselves, sanctuary rules are a symptom of a much broader disease: the nation's near-total loss of control over immigration policy. Fifty years ago immigration policy might have driven immigration numbers, but today the numbers drive policy. The nonstop increase of immigration is reshaping the language and the law to dissolve any distinction between legal and illegal aliens and, ultimately, the very idea of national borders.

It is a measure of how topsy-turvy the immigration environment has become that to ask police officials about the illegal-alien crime problem feels like a gross faux pas, not done in polite company. And a police official asked to violate this powerful taboo will give a strangled response—

or, as in the case of a New York deputy commissioner, break off communication altogether. Meanwhile millions of illegal aliens work, shop, travel, and commit crimes in plain view, utterly secure in their de facto immunity from the immigration law.

I asked the Miami Police Department's spokesman, Detective Delrish Moss, about his employer's policy on law-breaking illegals. In September 2004 the force arrested a Honduran visa violator for seven vicious rapes. The preceding year Miami cops had had the suspect in custody for lewd and lascivious molestation, without checking his immigration status. Had they done so, they would have discovered his visa overstay, a deportable offense, and so could have forestalled the rapes. "We have shied away from unnecessary involvement dealing with immigration issues," explains Moss, choosing his words carefully, "because of our large immigrant population."

Police commanders may not want to discuss, much less respond to, the illegal-alien crisis, but its magnitude for law enforcement is startling. Some examples:

• In Los Angeles, 95 percent of all outstanding warrants for homicide (which totaled twelve hundred to fifteen hundred) targeted illegal aliens. Up to two-thirds of all fugitive felony warrants (seventeen thousand) were for illegal aliens.

• A confidential California Department of Justice study reported in 1995 that 60 percent of the twenty-thousand-strong 18th Street Gang in southern California is illegal; police officers say the proportion is actually much greater. The bloody gang collaborates with the Mexican Mafia, the dominant force in California prisons, on complex drug-distribution schemes, extortion, and drive-by assassinations, and commits an assault or robbery every day in L.A. County. The gang has grown dramatically over the last two decades by recruiting recently arrived youngsters, most of them illegal, from Central America and Mexico.

• The leadership of the Colombia Lil' Cycos gang, which uses murder and racketeering to control the drug market around L.A.'s MacArthur Park, was about 60 percent illegal in 2002, says former assistant U.S. attorney Luis Li. Francisco Martinez, a Mexican Mafia member and an illegal alien, controlled the gang from prison while serving time for felonious reentry following deportation.

Good luck finding any reference to such facts in official crime analysis. In 2004, the LAPD and the L.A. city attorney requested an injunction against drug trafficking in Hollywood, targeting the 18th Street Gang and the "non–gang members" who sell drugs in Hollywood for the gang. Those non–gang members are virtually all illegal Mexicans, smuggled into the country by a ring organized by 18th Street bigs. The Mexicans pay off their transportation debts to the gang by selling drugs; many soon realize how lucrative that line of work is and stay in the business.

Cops and prosecutors universally know the immigration status of these non-gang "Hollywood dealers," as the city attorney calls them, but the gang injunction is assiduously silent on the matter. And if a Hollywood officer were to arrest an illegal dealer (known on the street as a "border brother") for his immigration status, or even notify the Immigration and Naturalization Service (since early 2003, absorbed into the new Department of Homeland Security), he would face severe discipline for violating Special Order 40, the city's sanctuary policy.

The ordinarily tough-as-nails former LAPD chief Daryl Gates enacted Special Order 40 in 1979—showing that even the most unapologetic law-and-order cop is no match for immigration advocates. The order prohibits officers from "initiating police action where the objective is to discover the alien status of a person"—in other words, the police may not even ask someone they have arrested about his immigration status until after they have filed criminal charges, nor may they arrest someone for immigration violations. They may not notify immigration authorities about an illegal alien picked up for minor violations. Only if they have already booked an illegal alien for a felony or for multiple misdemeanors may they inquire into his status or report him. The bottom line: a *cordon sanitaire* between local law enforcement and immigration authorities that creates a safe haven for illegal criminals.

L.A.'s sanctuary law and all others like it contradict a key 1990s policing discovery: the Great Chain of Being in criminal behavior. Pick up a law violator for a "minor" crime and you might well prevent a major crime: enforcing graffiti and turnstile-jumping laws nabs you murderers and robbers. Enforcing known immigration violations, such as reentry following deportation, against known felons, would be even more productive. LAPD officers recognize illegal deported gang members all the time—flashing gang signs at court hearings for rival gang-bangers, hanging out on the corner, or casing a target. These illegal returnees are, simply by being in the country after deportation, committing a felony (in contrast to garden-variety illegals on their first trip to the United States, say, who are only committing a misdemeanor). "But if I see a deportee from the Mara Salvatrucha [Salvadoran prison] gang crossing the street, I know I can't touch him," laments a Los Angeles gang officer. Only if the deported felon has given the officer some other reason to stop him, such as an observed narcotics sale, can the cop accost him—but not for the immigration felony.

Although such a policy puts the community at risk, the department's top brass brush off such concerns. No big deal if you see deported gangbangers back on the streets, they say. Just put them under surveillance for "real" crimes and arrest them for those. But surveillance is very manpower-intensive. Where there is an immediate ground for getting a violent felon off the street and for questioning him further, it is absurd to demand that the woefully understaffed LAPD ignore it.

In 2006, the department made a minor revision in Special Order 40: cops on the beat who see a deported felon may report it to their superiors, who then may, at their discretion, report the sighting to federal immigration agents. Needless to say, the gratuitous red tape all but guarantees that the illegal alien will be long gone if and when an Immigration and Customs Enforcement agent shows up to make an arrest.

The stated reasons for sanctuary policies are that they encourage illegal-alien crime victims and witnesses to cooperate with cops without fear of deportation, and that they encourage illegals to take advantage of city services like health care and education (to whose maintenance few illegals have contributed a single tax dollar, of course). There has never been any empirical verification that sanctuary laws actually accomplish these goals—and no one has ever suggested not enforcing drug laws, say, for fear of intimidating drug-using crime victims. But in any case, this official rationale could be honored by limiting police use of immigration laws to some subset of immigration violators: deported felons, say, or repeat criminal offenders whose immigration status police already know.

The real reason cities prohibit their cops and other employees from immigration reporting and enforcement is, like nearly everything else in immigration policy, the numbers. The immigrant population has grown so large that public officials are terrified of alienating it, even at the expense of ignoring the law and tolerating violence. In 1996 a breathtaking *Los Angeles Times* exposé on the 18th Street Gang, which included descriptions of innocent bystanders being murdered by laughing *cholos* (gang members), revealed the rate of illegal-alien membership in the gang. In response to the public outcry, the Los Angeles City Council ordered the police to reexamine Special Order 40. You would have thought it had suggested reconsidering *Roe v. Wade*. A police commander warned the council: "This is going to open a significant, heated debate." City Councilwoman Laura Chick put on a brave front: "We mustn't be afraid," she declared firmly.

But, of course, immigrant pandering trumped public safety. Law-abiding residents of gang-infested neighborhoods may live in terror of the tattooed gangbangers dealing drugs, spraying graffiti, and shooting up rivals outside their homes, but such anxiety can never equal a politician's fear of offending Hispanics. At the start of the reexamination process, LAPD deputy chief John White had argued that allowing the department to work closely with the INS would give cops another tool for getting gang members off the streets. Trying to build a homicide case, say, against an illegal gang member is often futile, he explained, since witnesses fear deadly retaliation if they cooperate with the police. Enforcing an immigration violation would allow the cops to lock up the murderer right now, without putting a witness's life at risk.

But six months later, Deputy Chief White had changed his tune: "Any broadening of the policy gets us into the immigration business," he asserted. "It's a federal law-enforcement issue, not a local law-enforcement issue." Interim police chief Bayan Lewis told the L.A. Police Commission: "It is not the time. It is not the day to look at Special Order 40."

Nor will it ever be, as long as immigration numbers continue to grow. After their brief moment of truth in 1996, Los Angeles politicians have only grown more adamant in defense of Special Order 40. After learning that cops in the scandal-plagued Rampart Division had cooperated with the INS to try to uproot murderous gang members from the community, local politicians threw a fit, criticizing district commanders for even allowing INS agents into their station houses. In turn, the LAPD strictly disciplined the offending officers. By now, big-city police chiefs are unfortunately just as determined to defend sanctuary policies as the politicians who appoint them; not so the rank and file, however, who see daily the benefit that an immigration tool would bring.

Immigration politics have similarly harmed New York. Former mayor Rudolph Giuliani sued all the way up to the Supreme Court to defend the city's sanctuary policy against a 1996 federal law decreeing that cities could not prohibit their employees from cooperating with the INS. Oh yeah? said Giuliani; just watch me. The INS, he claimed, with what turned out to be grotesque irony, only aims to "terrorize people." Although he lost in court, he remained defiant to the end. On September 5, 2001, his handpicked charter-revision committee ruled that New York could still require that its employees keep immigration information confidential to preserve trust between immigrants and government. Six days later, several visa-overstayers participated in the most devastating attack on the city and the country in history.

New York conveniently forgot the 1996 federal ban on sanctuary laws until a gang of five Mexicans—four of them illegal—abducted and brutally raped a forty-two-year-old mother of two near some railroad tracks in Queens. The NYPD had already arrested three of the illegal aliens numerous times for such crimes as assault, attempted robbery, criminal trespass, illegal gun possession, and drug offenses. The department had never notified the INS.

Citizen outrage forced Mayor Michael Bloomberg to revisit the city's sanctuary decree yet again. In May 2003 Bloomberg tweaked the policy minimally to allow city staffers to inquire into immigration status only if it is relevant to the awarding of a government benefit. Although Bloomberg's new rule said nothing about reporting immigration violations to federal officials, advocates immediately claimed that it did allow such reporting, and the ethnic lobbies went ballistic. "What we're seeing is the erosion of people's rights," thundered Angelo Falcon of the Puerto Rican Legal Defense and Education Fund. After three months of intense agitation by immigrant groups, Bloomberg replaced this innocuous "don't ask" policy with a "don't tell" rule even broader than Gotham's original sanctuary policy. The new rule prohibits city employees from giving other government officials information not just about immigration status but about tax payments, sexual orientation, welfare status, and other matters.

But even were immigrant-saturated cities to discard their sanctuary policies and begin enforcing immigration violations where public safety demands it, the resource-starved immigration authorities couldn't handle the overwhelming additional workload.

The chronic shortage of manpower to oversee, and detention space to house, aliens as they await their deportation hearings (or, following an order of removal from a federal judge, their actual deportation) has forced immigration officials to practice a constant triage. Long ago, the feds stopped trying to find and deport aliens who had "merely" entered the country illegally through stealth or fraudulent documents. Currently the only types of illegal aliens who run any risk of catching federal attention are those who have been convicted of an "aggravated felony" (a particularly egregious crime) or who have been deported following conviction for an aggravated felony and who have reentered (an offense punishable with twenty years in jail).

That triage has been going on for a long time, as former INS investigator Mike Cutler, who worked with the

NYPD catching Brooklyn drug dealers in the 1970s, explains. "If you arrested someone you wanted to detain, you'd go to your boss and start a bidding war," Cutler recalls. "You'd say: 'My guy ran three blocks, threw a couple of punches, and had six pieces of ID.' The boss would turn to another agent: 'Next! Whaddid your guy do?' 'He ran eighteen blocks, pushed over an old lady, and had a gun.'" But such one-upmanship was usually fruitless. "Without the jail space," explains Cutler, "it was like the Fish and Wildlife Service; you'd tag their ear and let them go."

But even when immigration officials actually arrest someone, and even if a judge issues a final deportation order (usually after years of litigation and appeals), they rarely have the manpower to put the alien on a bus or plane and take him across the border. Second alternative: detain him pending removal. Again, inadequate space and staff. In the early 1990s, for example, 15 INS officers were in charge of the deportation of approximately 85,000 aliens (not all of them criminals) in New York City. The agency's actual response to final orders of removal was what is known as a "run letter"—a notice asking the deportable alien kindly to show up in a month or two to be deported, when the agency might be able to process him. Results: in 2001, 87 percent of deportable aliens who received run letters disappeared, a number that was even higher—94 percent—if they were from terror-sponsoring countries.

To other law-enforcement agencies, the feds' triage often looks like complete indifference to immigration violations. Testifying to Congress about the Queens rape by illegal Mexicans, New York's criminal justice coordinator defended the city's failure to notify the INS after the rapists' previous arrests on the ground that the agency wouldn't have responded anyway. "We have time and time again been unable to reach INS on the phone," John Feinblatt said in February 2004. "When we reach them on the phone, they require that we write a letter. When we write a letter, they require that it be by a superior."

Criminal aliens also interpret the triage as indifference. John Mullaly, a former NYPD homicide detective, estimates that 70 percent of the drug dealers and other criminals in Manhattan's Washington Heights were illegal. Were Mullaly to threaten an illegal-alien thug in custody that his next stop would be El Salvador unless he cooperated, the criminal would just laugh, knowing that the INS would never show up. The message could not be clearer: this is a culture that can't enforce its most basic law of entry. If policing's broken-windows theory is correct, the failure to enforce one set of rules breeds overall contempt for the law.

The sheer number of criminal aliens overwhelmed an innovative program that would allow immigration officials to complete deportation hearings while a criminal was still in state or federal prison, so that upon his release he could be immediately ejected without taking up precious INS detention space. But the process, begun in 1988, immediately bogged down due to the numbers—in 2000, for example, nearly 30 percent of federal prisoners were foreign-born. The agency couldn't find enough pro bono attorneys to represent such an army of criminal aliens (who have extensive due-process rights in contesting deportation) and so would have to request delay after delay. Or enough immigration judges would not be available. In 1997 the INS simply had no record of a whopping 36 percent of foreign-born inmates who had been released from federal and four state prisons without any review of their deportability. They included 1,198 aggravated felons, 80 of whom were soon rearrested for new crimes.

Resource starvation is not the only reason for federal inaction. The INS was a creature of immigration politics, and INS district directors came under great pressure from local politicians to divert scarce resources into distribution of such "benefits" as permanent residency, citizenship, and work permits, and away from criminal or other investigations. In the late 1980s, for example, the INS refused to join an FBI task force against Haitian drug trafficking in Miami, fearing criticism for "Haitian-bashing." In 1997, after Hispanic activists protested a much-publicized raid that netted nearly two dozen illegals, the border patrol said it would no longer join Simi Valley, California, probation officers on home searches of illegal-alien-dominated gangs.

The disastrous Citizenship USA project of 1996 was a luminous case of politics driving the INS to sacrifice enforcement to "benefits." When, in the early 1990s, the prospect of welfare reform drove immigrants to apply for citizenship in record numbers to preserve their welfare eligibility, the Clinton administration, seeing a political bonanza in hundreds of thousands of new welfare-dependent citizens, ordered the naturalization process radically expedited. Thanks to relentless administration pressure, processing errors in 1996 were 99 percent in New York and 90 percent in Los Angeles, and tens of thousands of aliens with criminal records, including for murder and armed robbery, were naturalized.

Another powerful political force, the immigration bar association, has won from Congress an elaborate set of due-process rights for criminal aliens that can keep them in the country indefinitely. In 2004, federal probation officers in Brooklyn were supervising two illegals—a Jordanian and an Egyptian with Saudi citizenship—who looked "ready to blow up the Statue of Liberty," according to a probation official, but the officers couldn't get rid of them. The Jordanian had been caught fencing stolen Social Security and tax-refund checks; now he sells phone cards, which he uses himself to make untraceable calls. The Saudi's offense: using a fraudulent Social Security number to get employment—a puzzlingly unnecessary scam, since he receives large sums from the Middle East, including from millionaire relatives. But intelligence links him to terrorism, so presumably he worked in order not to draw attention to himself. Currently he changes his cell phone every month. Ordinarily such a minor offense would not be prosecuted, but the government, fearing he had terrorist intentions, used whatever it had to put him in prison.

Now probation officers desperately want to see the duo out of the country, but the two ex-cons have hired lawyers, who are relentlessly fighting their deportation. "Due process allows you to stay for years without an adjudication," says a probation officer in frustration. "A regular immigration attorney can keep you in the country for three years, a high-priced one for ten." In the meantime, Brooklyn probation officials are watching the bridges.

Even where immigration officials successfully nab and deport criminal aliens, the reality, says a former federal gang prosecutor, is that "they all come back. They can't make it in Mexico." The tens of thousands of illegal farmworkers and dishwashers who overpower U.S. border controls every year carry in their wake thousands of brutal assailants and terrorists who use the same smuggling industry and who benefit from the same irresistible odds: there are so many more of them than the border patrol.

For, of course, the government's inability to keep out criminal aliens is part and parcel of its inability to patrol the border, period. For decades the INS had as much effect on the migration of millions of illegals as a can tied to the tail of a tiger. And the immigrants themselves, despite the press cliché of hapless aliens living fearfully in the shadows, seemed to regard immigration authorities with all the concern of an elephant for a flea.

Certainly fear of immigration officers is not in evidence among the hundreds of illegal day laborers who hang out on Roosevelt Avenue in Queens, New York, in front of money-wire services, travel agencies, immigration-attorney offices, and phone arcades, all catering to the local Hispanic population (as well as to drug dealers and terrorists). "There is no chance of getting caught," cheerfully explains Rafael, an Ecuadoran. Like the dozen Ecuadorans and Mexicans on his particular corner, Rafael is hoping that an SUV seeking carpenters for $100 a day will show up soon. "We don't worry, because we're not doing anything wrong. I know it's illegal; I need the papers, but here, nobody asks you for papers."

Even the newly fortified Mexican border, the one spot where the government really tries to prevent illegal immigration, looms as only a minor inconvenience to the day laborers. The odds, they realize, are overwhelmingly in their favor. Miguel, a reserved young carpenter, crossed the border at Tijuana three years ago with 15 others. Border patrol spotted them, but with six officers to 16 illegals, only five got caught. In illegal border crossings, you get what you pay for, Miguel says. If you try to shave on the fee, the coyotes [the smugglers who are leading your group] will abandon you at the first problem. Miguel's wife was flying into New York from Los Angeles that very day; it had cost him $2,200 to get her across the border. "Because I pay, I don't worry," he says complacently.

The only way to dampen illegal immigration and its attendant train of criminals and terrorists—short of an economic revolution in the sending countries or an impregnably militarized border—is to remove the jobs magnet. As long as migrants know they can easily get work, they will find ways to evade border controls. But enforcing laws against illegal labor is among government's lowest priorities. In 2001 only 124 agents nationwide were trying to find and prosecute the hundreds of thousands of employers and millions of illegal aliens who violate the employment laws, the Associated Press reports.

Even were immigration officials to devote adequate resources to worksite investigations, not much would change, because their legal weapons are so weak. That's no accident: though it is a crime to hire illegal aliens, a coalition of libertarians, business lobbies, and left-wing advocates has consistently blocked the fraud-proof form of work authorization necessary to enforce that ban. Libertarians have erupted in hysteria at such proposals as a toll-free number to the Social Security Administration for employers to confirm Social Security numbers. Hispanics warn just as stridently that helping employers verify work eligibility would result in discrimination against Hispanics—implicitly conceding that vast numbers of Hispanics work illegally.

The result: hiring practices in illegal-immigrant-saturated industries are a charade. Millions of illegal workers pretend to present valid documents, and thousands of employers pretend to believe them. The law doesn't require the employer to verify that a worker is actually qualified to work, and as long as the proffered documents are not patently phony—scrawled with red crayon on a matchbook, say—the employer will nearly always be exempt from liability merely by having eyeballed them. To find an employer guilty of violating the ban on hiring illegal aliens, immigration authorities must prove that he knew he was getting fake papers—an almost insurmountable burden. Meanwhile the market for counterfeit documents has exploded: in one month alone in 1998, immigration authorities seized nearly two million of them in Los Angeles, destined for immigrant workers, welfare seekers, criminals, and terrorists.

For illegal workers and employers, there is no downside to the employment charade. If immigration officials ever do try to conduct an industry-wide investigation—which will at least net the illegal employees, if not the employers—local congressmen will almost certainly head it off. An INS inquiry into the Vidalia onion industry in Georgia was not only aborted by Georgia's congressional delegation, it actually resulted in a local amnesty for the growers' illegal workforce. The downside to complying with the spirit of the employment law, on the other hand, is considerable. Ethnic advocacy groups are ready to picket employers who dismiss illegal workers, and employers understandably fear being undercut by less scrupulous competitors.

Of the incalculable changes in American politics, demographics, and culture that the continuing surge of migrants is causing, one of the most profound is the breakdown of the distinction between legal and illegal entry. Everywhere illegal aliens receive free public education and free medical care at taxpayer expense; thirteen states offer them driver's licenses. States everywhere have been pushed to grant illegal aliens college scholarships and reduced in-state tuition. One hundred banks, more than eight hundred law-enforcement agencies, and dozens of cities accept an identification card created by Mexico to credentialize illegal Mexican aliens in the United States. The Bush administration has given its blessing to this *matricula consular* card over the strong protest of the FBI, which warns that the gaping security loopholes that the card creates make it a boon to money launderers, immigrant smugglers, and terrorists. Border authorities have already caught an Iranian man sneaking across the border this year, Mexican *matricula* card in hand.

Hispanic advocates have helped blur the distinction between a legal and an illegal resident by asserting that differentiating the two is an act of irrational bigotry. Arrests of illegal aliens inside the border now inevitably spark protests, often led by the Mexican government, that feature signs calling for *"no más racismo."* Immigrant advocates use the language of "human rights" to appeal to an authority higher than such trivia as citizenship laws. They attack the term "amnesty" for implicitly acknowledging the validity of borders. Indeed, grouses Illinois congressman Luís Gutiérrez, "There's an implication that somehow you did something wrong and you need to be forgiven."

Illegal aliens and their advocates speak loudly about what they think the United States owes them, not vice versa. "I believe they have a right . . . to work, to drive their kids to school," said California assemblywoman Sarah Reyes. An immigration agent says that people he stops "get in your face about their rights, because our failure to enforce the law emboldens them." Taking this idea to its extreme, Joaquín Avila, a UCLA Chicano studies professor and law lecturer, argues that to deny non-citizens the vote, especially in the many California cities where they constitute the majority, is a form of apartheid.

Yet no poll has ever shown that Americans want more open borders. Quite the reverse. By a huge majority—at least 60 percent—they want to rein in immigration, and they endorse an observation that Senator Alan Simpson made twenty years ago: Americans "are fed up with efforts to make them feel that [they] do not have that fundamental right of any people—to decide who will join them and help form the future country in which they and their posterity will live." But if the elites' and the advocates' idea of giving voting rights to non-citizen majorities catches on— and don't be surprised if it does—Americans could be faced with the ultimate absurdity of people outside the social compact making rules for those inside it.

However the nation ultimately decides to rationalize its chaotic and incoherent immigration system, surely all can agree that, at a minimum, authorities should expel illegal-alien criminals swiftly. Even on the grounds of protecting non-criminal illegal immigrants, we should start by junking sanctuary policies. By stripping cops of what may be their only immediate tool to remove felons from the community, these policies leave law-abiding immigrants prey to crime.

But the non-enforcement of immigration laws in general has an even more destructive effect. In many immigrant communities, assimilation into gangs seems to be outstripping assimilation into civic culture. Toddlers are learning to flash gang signals and hate the police, reports the *Los Angeles Times*. In New York City, "every high school has its Mexican gang," and most twelve- to fourteen-year-olds have already joined, claims Ernesto Vega, an illegal eighteen-year-old Mexican. Such pathologies only worsen when the first lesson that immigrants learn about U.S. law is that Americans don't bother to enforce it. "Institutionalizing illegal immigration creates a mindset in people that anything goes in the U.S.," observes Patrick Ortega, the news and public-affairs director of Radio Nueva Vida in southern California. "It creates a new subculture, with a sequela of social ills." It is broken windows writ large.

For the sake of immigrants and native-born Americans alike, it's time to decide what our immigration policy is—and enforce it.

5

HEATHER MAC DONALD

The Immigrant Gang Plague

Before immigration optimists issue another rosy prognosis for America's multicultural future, they might visit Belmont High School in Los Angeles's overwhelmingly Hispanic, gang-ridden Rampart Division. "Upward and onward" is not a phrase that comes to mind when speaking to the first- and second-generation immigrant teens milling around the school this January.

"Most of the people I used to hang out with when I first came to the school have dropped out," observes Jackie, a vivacious illegal alien from Guatemala. "Others got kicked out or got into drugs. Five graduated, and four homegirls got pregnant."

Certainly, none of the older teens I met outside Belmont was on track to graduate. Jackie herself flunked ninth grade ("I used to ditch a lot," she explains) and never caught up. She is now pursuing a General Equivalency Diploma—a watered-down certificate for dropouts or expelled students—in the school's "adult" division. Vanessa, who sports a tiny horseshoe protruding from her nostrils, is applying to the adult division, too, having been kicked out of Belmont at age eighteen. "I didn't come to school very often," says this American-born child of illegal aliens from El Salvador. Her boyfriend, Albert, a dashing nineteen-year-old with long, slicked-back hair, got expelled for truancy but has talked his way back into the regular high school. "I have good manipulative skills," he smiles. After a robbery conviction, Albert was put on probation but broke every rule in the book: "Curfews, grades, attendance, missed court days," he boasts. "But they still let me off the hook."

These Belmont teens are no aberration. Hispanic youths, whether recent arrivals or birthright American citizens, are developing an underclass culture. (By "Hispanic" here, I mean the population originating in Latin America—above all, in Mexico—as distinct from America's much smaller Puerto Rican and Dominican communities of Caribbean descent, which have themselves long shown elevated crime and welfare rates.) Hispanic school dropout rates and teen birthrates are now the highest in the nation. Gang crime is exploding nationally—rising 50 percent from 1999 to 2002—driven by the march of Hispanic immigration east and north across the country. Most worrisome, underclass indicators like crime and single parenthood do not improve over successive generations of Hispanics—they worsen.

Debate has recently heated up over whether Mexican immigration—unique in its scale and in other important ways—will defeat the American tradition of assimilation. The rise of underclass behavior among the progeny of Mexicans and other Central Americans must be part of that debate. There may be assimilation going on, but a significant portion of it is assimilation downward to the worst elements of American life. To be sure, most Hispanics are hardworking, law-abiding residents; they have reclaimed squalid neighborhoods in South Central Los Angeles and elsewhere. Among the dozens of Hispanic youths I interviewed, several expressed gratitude for the United States, a sentiment that would be hard to find among the ordinary run of teenagers. But given the magnitude of present immigration levels, if only a portion of those from south of the border goes bad, the costs to society will be enormous.

The Soledad Enrichment Action Charter School in South Central Los Angeles is at the vortex of L.A.'s gang culture. Next door to a rose-colored, angel-bedecked church, the boxy school glowers behind barred gates like those that surround prisons. Soledad's students, about half blacks and half Hispanics, have been kicked out of other schools. They have brought violence with them. In early March, a gunman opened fire on twenty students entering the school at 7:30 a.m., wounding two. Tensions were high again as school let out one day in April. A boy had been sent home earlier for fighting; the question now was, would he return to retaliate? The school's probation officer radioed the LAPD's 77th Division to plead for some officers to keep watch, without success. As the students, dressed in plain white T-shirts, filed out to the sidewalk, two burly security guards and a gang counselor warily eyed the street.

Asked about gangs, the teens proudly reel off their affiliations: SOK (Still Out Killing); HTO (Hispanics Taking Over); JMC (Just Mobbing Crazy). A cocky American-born child of Salvadoran parents says that most of his peers from the eighth grade are "locked up or dead." "Four are dead—three were shot, one was run over." Were you just lucky? I ask. "They were gangbanging more than me," says the seventeen-year-old, who won't give his name. "I try to control myself, respect my parents." That respect only goes so far. Asked if he's been in jail, he swaggers: "Yup, for GTA"—grand theft auto. And he has no intention of leaving his gang: "They're the homeys, part of the family."

Eighteen-year-old Eric, born here to an illegal Mexican and Guatemalan, is one of the few students I talked to who doesn't gangbang, though he is on probation for second-degree robbery, his second conviction. Half his friends from elementary school are involved in crime, he says. Of course, gang problems in Los Angeles schools are hardly confined to academies for delinquents like Soledad. Gang fights in some of L.A.'s regular high schools draw such crowds that youthful pickpockets have a field day working the spectators and participants. "People would steal your pagers and cell phones," reports one student who has bounced through several schools.

David O'Connell, pastor of the church next door to Soledad, has been fighting L.A.'s gang culture for over a decade. He rues the "ferocious stuff" that is currently coming out of Central America, sounding weary and pessimistic. But "what's more frightening," he says, "is the disengagement from adults." Hispanic children feel they have to deal with problems themselves, apart from their parents, according to O'Connell, and they "do so in violent ways." The adults, for their part, start to fear young people, including their own children.

The pull to a culture of violence among Hispanic children begins earlier and earlier, O'Connell says. Researchers and youth workers across the country confirm his observation. In Chicago, gangs start recruiting kids at age nine, according to criminologists studying policing and social trends in the Windy City. The Chicago Community Policing Evaluation Consortium concluded that gangs have become fully integrated into Hispanic youth culture; even children not in gangs emulate their attitudes, dress, and self-presentation. The result is a community in thrall. Non-affiliated children fear traveling into unknown neighborhoods and sometimes drop out of school for lack of protection. Adults are just as scared. They may know who has been spray-painting their garage, for example, but won't tell the police for fear their car will be torched in retaliation. "It's like we're in our own little jails that we can't leave," said a resident. "There isn't an uninfested place nearby."

Washington, D.C., reports the same "ever-younger" phenomenon. "Recruitment is starting early in middle school," says Lori Kaplan, head of D.C.'s Latin American Youth Center. With early recruitment comes a high school dropout rate of 50 percent. "Gang culture is gaining more recruits than our ability to get kids out," Kaplan laments. "We can get this kid out, but two or three will take his place." In May 2004, an eighteen-year-old member of the Salvadoran Mara Salvatrucha gang used a machete to chop off four left fingers and nearly sever the right hand of a sixteen-year-old South Side Locos rival in the Washington suburbs.

Ernesto Vega, a nineteen-year-old Mexican illegal who grew up in New York City, estimates that most twelve- to fourteen-year-old Mexicans and Mexican Americans in New York are in gangs for protection. "If you're Mexican, you can't go to parties by yourself," he says. "People will ask, 'Who you down with? *Que barrio?*' They be checkin' you out. But if it's twenty of you, and twenty of them, then it's OK."

For some children the choice is: get beat up once a week, or get beat up once to enter the gang. Others join for the prestige and sense of belonging. Mario Flores was one of them; he joined Santa Ana, California's, Westside Compadres. "When I was thirteen, I was like, 'Wow.' I wanted them to jump me," he says in the soft near-whisper of the cool. "They're like, 'You want to get down?' They got to jumping at you, they go to call you, 'Trips from Westside Comps'—you feel good."

Flores (or "Trips") is a depressing specimen of gang culture: uneducated and barely articulate. He's sitting on the other side of a Plexiglas window in the Santa Ana Central Jail, talking to me over a phone. In and out of jail with dazzling regularity over the last three years, he most recently left prison on April 14, 2004. A week later, he was arrested again on a rape charge. Born in Portland, Oregon, but raised in Mexico, Flores went to live with cousins in San Bernardino, California, at age thirteen and has been traveling the Southern California gang circuit—Riverside

County, Santa Ana, East L.A.—ever since. Now twenty, he is slender and finely chiseled. Gang hand gestures accompany his speech like hieroglyphics. "When I saw gang members," he says, pointing first to his eyes, then outward, "they're like, 'Are you down with my shit?' 'I'm down!'" I ask if he speaks English or Spanish with his gang. "You speak Chicano," he says. "'Hey, homey!' You mostly talk English, you've got some good words. But the way you talk, you don't talk good. You don't talk like other people."

Flores expresses the fierce attachment to territory that is the sine qua non of gang identity. "I was like, 'I love my neighborhood. If you don't love my neighborhood, I'm going to fuck you up.'" Charles Beck, captain of the LAPD's Rampart Division, marvels at this emotion. "They all come from identical neighborhoods, identical families, and go to identical schools, and yet they hate each other with a passion." The territorial instincts can only be compared to the Balkans, says Corporal Kevin Ruiz, a Santa Ana gang investigator. "There's people who all they do is patrol gang boundaries. They're like me, in a way: I'm looking for bad guys; they look for rivals."

"Trips" showed his love for Santa Ana's Westside Compadres by doing "missions"—robbing bars, stealing wallets and cell phones, selling drugs—to raise money for the gang. "If a big homey told me to fuck someone up, I had to," he explains. The gang reciprocated by giving him a place to stay—when he was bringing in cash. Otherwise he lived in cars or on the street, sometimes in a hotel.

The chance that Flores will ever become a productive member of society is slight. Routinely kicked out of high school for fighting, he lacks rudimentary skills. Like many prisoners, he claims to be reading the Bible and thanking Jesus, but such prison conversions rarely last. His personal life is troubled: "My lady, she mad at me"—not surprisingly, given his most recent rape charge—and Flores is not certain she will be waiting for him when he gets out of jail. Most likely, Flores will continue contributing to the Hispanicization of prisons in California: in 1970, Hispanics were 12 percent of the state's population and 16 percent of new prison admits; by 1998 they were 30 percent of the California population, and 42 percent of new admits.

Even as it reaches down to ever-younger recruits, gang culture is growing more lethal. In April 2004, sixteen-year-old Valentino Arenas drove up to a courthouse in Pomona, California, and shot to death a randomly chosen California Highway Patrol officer, in the hope of gaining entry to Pomona's 12th Street Gang. The assassination wouldn't surprise Dennis Farrell, a Nassau County, New York, homicide detective. "We're amazed at the openness of shootings," he says. "When we do cases with Hispanic gangs, we often get full statements of admission, almost like they don't see what's the big deal."

The unwritten code that moderated gang violence three or four decades ago has now fallen away. "When I grew up," says Santa Ana native and gang investigator Kevin Ruiz, "there were rules of engagement: no shooting at churches or at home. Now, no one is immune." One of Ruiz's colleagues on the Santa Ana police force, Mona Ruiz (no relation), spent her adolescence in Santa Ana gangs; now she tries to get kids out. "Back then," she says, "if someone got jumped, you responded with fistfights, not guns. Guns started in the 1980s." Earlier gangbangers even showed a certain fastidiousness of dress: "Guys used to iron their jeans for two hours," Mona Ruiz recalls. "Then they wouldn't sit down" to avoid marring the crease. All that changed when heroin hit, she says.

The constant invasion of illegal aliens is worsening gang violence as well. In Phoenix, Arizona, and surrounding Maricopa County, illegal-alien gangs, such as Brown Pride and Wetback Power, are growing more volatile and dangerous, according to Tom Bearup, a former sheriff's department official and current candidate for sheriff. Even in prison, where they clash with American Hispanics, they are creating a more vicious environment.

Upward mobility to the suburbs doesn't necessarily break the allure of gang culture. An immigration agent reports that in the middle-class suburbs of southwest Miami, second- and third-generation Hispanic youths are perpetrating home invasions, robberies, battery, drug sales, and rape. Kevin Ruiz knows students at the University of California, Irvine, who retain their gang connections. Prosecutors in formerly crime-free Ventura County, California, sought an injunction in May 2004 against the Colonia Chiques gang after homicides rocketed up; an affidavit supporting the injunction details how Chiques members terrorize the local hospital whenever one of the gang arrives with a gunshot wound. Federal law-enforcement officials in Virginia are tracking with alarm the spread of gang violence from Northern Virginia west into the Shenandoah Valley and south toward Charlottesville, a trend so disturbing that they secured federal funds in May 2004 to stanch the mayhem. "This is beyond a regional problem. It is, in fact, a national problem," said FBI assistant director Michael Mason, head of the bureau's Washington field office.

Open-borders apologists dismiss the Hispanic crime threat by observing that black crime rates are even higher. True, but irrelevant: the black population is not growing, whereas Hispanic immigration is reaching virtually every part of the country, sometimes radically changing local demographics. With a felony arrest rate up to triple that of whites, Hispanics can dramatically raise community crime levels.

Many cops and youth workers blame the increase in gang appeal on the disintegration of the Hispanic family. The trends are worsening, especially for U.S.-born Hispanics. In California, 67 percent of children of U.S.-born Hispanic parents lived in an intact family in 1990; by 1999 that number had dropped to 56 percent. The percentage of Hispanic children living with a single mother in California rose from 18 percent in 1990 to 29 percent in 1999. Nationally, single-parent households constituted 25 percent of all Hispanic households with minor children in 1980; by 2000 the proportion had jumped to 34 percent.

The trends in teen parenthood—the marker of underclass behavior—will almost certainly affect the crime and gang rate. Hispanics now outrank blacks for teen births; Mexican teens have higher birthrates than Puerto Ricans, previously the most "ghettoized" Hispanic subgroup in terms of welfare use and out-of-wedlock child-rearing. In 2002 there were 83.4 births per 1,000 Hispanic females between ages 15 and 19, compared with 66.6 among blacks, 28.5 among non-Hispanic whites, and 18.3 among Asians.

Perhaps these young Hispanic mothers are giving birth as wives? Unlikely. In California, where Latina teens have the highest birthrate of teens in any state, 79 percent of teen births to U.S.-born Latinas in 1999 were to unmarried girls.

According to the many young Hispanics I spoke to, more and more girls are getting pregnant. "This year was the worst for pregnancies," says Liliana, an American-born senior at Manual Arts High School near downtown Los Angeles. "A lot of girls get abortions; some drop out." Are girls ashamed when they get pregnant? I wonder. "Not at all," Liliana responds. Among Hispanic teens, at least, if not among their parents, the stigma of single parenthood has vanished. I asked Jackie, the Guatemalan GED student at L.A.'s Belmont High, if her pregnant friends subsequently got married. She guffawed. George, an eighteen-year-old of Salvadoran background who was kicked out of Manual Arts six months ago for a vicious fight, estimates that most girls at the school are having sex by age sixteen.

Mexican and Central American immigration to New York City is of much more recent vintage than in California, but young Mexicans in New York have quickly assimilated to underclass sexual behavior. Nineteen-year-old Ernesto Vega reports that his oldest sister dropped out of school at seventeen and got pregnant the next year. "I heard her boyfriend came from Mexico to work, but he wasn't working. He was on the street," Ernesto says. Then the boyfriend got arrested, probably on drug charges. "He says he was arrested for doing nothing, but they don't arrest you for doing nothing."

Ernesto knows three or four Mexican-American girls with babies, including a sixteen-year-old with two daughters. "Another just got pregnant this year," he says. "She's fifteen." None is married. None has a GED or will go to college. As for the fathers of their children? "The boys be leaving the girls alone," Vega says. "The boy goes away."

Some Hispanic parents valiantly try to impose old-fashioned consequences on teen pregnancies, but they are losing the battle. Vega's father, a building superintendent and hardware store clerk, angrily told his pregnant daughter, according to Vega: "You gotta go live with [the boyfriend]. I now want nothing to do with you!" The boyfriend offered to take the girl into the apartment he was sharing with a female acquaintance, but she wanted her own place. Eventually she persuaded her father to take her back, but only on the condition that she work. She now sells Yankee paraphernalia on the Grand Concourse in the Bronx.

Traditional and contemporary family values continued to clash throughout the pregnancy. Although the boyfriend vanished until the birth, he showed up at Vega's house with his whole family when the girl returned from the hospital with her newborn. "He took his three sisters and his mother; one sister took the nephews," Vega recalls. The boyfriend's demand: you have to decide where to live. The girl told him to take a hike. The family delegation, Vega judges, already adapting to American individualist norms, was inappropriate. "The problem was not with the families," he says, "but between him and her."

In one respect, Central American immigrants break the mold of traditional American underclass behavior: they work. Even so, Mexican welfare receipt is twice as high as that of natives, in large part because Mexican-American incomes are so low, and remain low over successive generations. Disturbingly, welfare dependency actually rises between the second and third generation—to 31 percent of all third-generation Mexican-American households. Illegal Hispanics make liberal use of welfare, too, by putting their American-born children on public assistance: in Orange County, California, nearly twice as many Hispanic welfare cases are for children of illegal aliens as for legal families.

More troublingly, some Hispanics combine work with gangbanging. Gang detectives in Long Island's Suffolk County know when members of the violent Salvadoran MS-13 gang get off work from their lawn-maintenance or pizzeria jobs, and can follow them to their gang meetings. Mexican gang members in rural Pennsylvania, which saw two gang homicides in late April 2004 also often work in landscaping and construction.

On the final component of underclass behavior—school failure—Hispanics are in a class by themselves. No other group drops out in greater numbers. In Los Angeles only 48 percent of Hispanic ninth-graders graduate, compared with a 56 percent citywide graduation rate and a 70 percent nationwide rate. In 2000 nearly 30 percent of Hispanics between the ages of sixteen and twenty-four were high school dropouts nationwide, compared with about 13 percent of blacks and about 7 percent of whites.

The constant inflow of barely literate recent Mexican arrivals unquestionably brings down Hispanic education levels. But later American-born generations don't brighten the picture much. While Mexican Americans make significant education gains between the first and second generation, adding three and a half years of schooling, progress stalls in the next generation, economists Jeffrey Grogger and Stephen Trejo have found. Third-generation Mexican Americans remain three times as likely to drop out of high school than whites and one and a half times as likely to drop out as blacks. They complete college at one-third the rate of whites. Mexican Americans are assimilating not to the national schooling average, observed the Federal Reserve Bank of Dallas this June, but to the dramatically lower "Hispanic average." In educational outcomes, concluded the bank, "Ethnicity matters."

No one knows why this is so. Every parent I spoke to said that she wanted her children to do well in school and go to college. Yet the message is often not getting across. "Hispanic parents are the kind of parents that leave it to others," explains an unwed Salvadoran welfare mother in Santa Ana. "We don't get that involved." A news director of a southern California Spanish radio station expresses frustration at the passivity toward education and upward mobility he sees in his own family. "I tried to knock the 'Spanglish' accent out of my niece and get rid of that crap," he says. "But the mother was completely nihilistic about her child. It's going to take direct action from Americans to Americanize Hispanics."

Perhaps the answer to the disconnect between stated parental goals and educational outcomes lies in Hispanic culture's traditional suspicion of education. Santa Ana police officer Mona Ruiz recounts a joke told by comedian George Lopez: "When a white person graduates, people say, 'You did good.' When a Mexican graduates, people say, 'You think you're better than us.'" The lure of an immediate income often proves more compelling than a four- to eight-year investment in self-improvement. New Yorker Ernesto Vega says he knows "Mexicans with papers" who drop out of high school. "They young. They say, 'I'm going to start working, I don't need school.'" But Vega has no illusions about the consequences: "Even with papers, you're only making $300 a week as a delivery boy in restaurants, because you don't know anything else."

Proponents of unregulated immigration simply ignore the growing underclass problem among later generations of Hispanics, with its attendant gang involvement and teen pregnancy. When pressed, open-borders advocates dismiss worries about the Hispanic future with their favorite comparison between Mexicans and Italians. Popularized by political analyst Michael Barone in *The New Americans*, the analogy goes like this: a century ago, Italian immigrants anticipated the Mexican influx, above all in their disregard for education. They dropped out of school in high numbers—yet they eventually prospered and joined the mainstream. Therefore, argue Barone and others, Mexicans will too.

But the analogy is flawed. To begin with, the magnitude of Mexican immigration renders all historical comparisons irrelevant, as Harvard historian Samuel Huntington argues in his latest book, *Who Are We?* In 2000, Mexicans constituted nearly 30 percent of the foreign-born population in the United States; the next two largest groups were the Chinese (5 percent) and Filipinos (4 percent). By contrast, at the turn of the twentieth century the largest immigrant group, Germans, made up only 15 percent of the foreign-born population. In 1910, Great Britain, Germany, Ireland, and Italy, in that order, sent the most migrants to the United States; Italians made up only 17 percent of the combined total. English speakers made up more than half the new arrivals; there was no chance that Italian would become the dominant language in any part of the country. By contrast, half of today's immigrants speak Spanish.

Equally important, the flow of newcomers came to an abrupt halt after World War I and did not resume until 1965. This long pause allowed the country ample opportunity to Americanize the foreign-born and their children. Today no end is in sight to the migration from Mexico and its neighbors, which continually reinforces Mexican culture in American Hispanic communities and seems likely to do so for decades into the future.

Contemporary Hispanic immigration also differs from the classic Ellis Island model in that the ease of cross-border travel and communication allows Mexican and Central American immigrants to keep at least one foot planted in their native land. Meanwhile the Mexican government does everything it can to bind Mexican migrants psychologically to the home country, in order to safeguard the annual $24 billion flow of remittances, a figure confirmed by the Bank of Mexico. It encourages dual nationality, and Mexicans in the United States can now run for office in Mexico. A Yolo County, California, tomato farmer has already been elected mayor of Jerez. Not surprisingly, Mexicans and other Central Americans have the lowest rates of naturalization of all immigrants—less than 30 percent in 1990, compared with two-thirds of qualified immigrants from major European sending countries, the Philippines, and Hong Kong.

Even Mexico's former foreign minister, Jorge Castañeda, acknowledges the unprecedented character of Hispanic immigration. "Mexican immigration," he wrote recently, "does have distinctive traits that do make [assimilation] difficult, if not impossible. This is . . . a matter of history." That "history" holds that the United States robbed Mexico of its natural territory in the nineteenth century, as some Mexican immigrants never seem to forget. "It's kind of scary," says Santa Ana gang intervention officer Mona Ruiz. "I hear, 'I was here first; this used to be Mexico. You stole it from us.'" Mexican-American Ruiz is herself called a "traitor" for becoming Americanized.

While proponents of the "reconquista" of "Alta California" (as Mexican nationalists call the lost territory) are a small minority of Hispanic immigrants, a much larger proportion hold on to their Hispanic identities. Few of the American-born students I spoke to in southern California identified themselves as "American." Many said they were "Mexican," "Latino," or "Mexican American"—usages encouraged by the multicultural dogma in the schools, a far cry from the Americanization efforts of classrooms a century ago.

Michael Barone's Italian-Mexican comparison also ignores the differences between the U.S. economies of 1904 and 2004. While Italian dropouts in 1904 could make their way into the middle class by working in the booming manufacturing sector or by plying their existing craftsman skills, that is far more difficult today, given the decline of factory jobs and the rise of the knowledge-based economy. As the limited education of Mexican Americans depresses their wages, their sense of being stuck in an economic backwater breeds resentment. "The second generation becomes angry with America, as they see their fathers faltering," observes César Barrios, an outreach worker for the Tepeyac Association, a social-services agency for Mexicans in New York City. This resentment only increases the lure of underclass culture, with its rebellious rejection of conventional norms, according to Barrios. For this reason, he says, many young Mexicans "prefer to imitate blacks rather than white people."

The Spanish-language media, which reaches two-thirds of all Hispanics, reinforces the sense of grievance. Stories about America's cruelties to immigrants and the country's shocking failure to legalize illegal aliens dominate news coverage. A billboard for Los Angeles's Spanish newspaper *La Opinión* conveys the usual tone: "Justice," "Abuse," "Deportation," and other hot-button topics blare out in massive lettering.

Chicago provides a cautionary tale about high levels of Hispanic immigration combined with an ever more powerful underclass ethic. In the 1990s the Hispanic population in Chicago grew 38 percent, to 754,000, and became increasingly concentrated in the city's barrios. Education levels and fluency in English dropped lower and lower while serious crime, social disorder, and physical decay grew in direct proportion to the number of Spanish-speaking Latinos. After a neighborhood became more than 60 percent Latino, physical decay—including graffiti, trash-filled vacant lots, and abandoned cars—jumped disproportionately. By 2001 social pathology among Spanish-speaking Latinos was higher than for any other racial or ethnic group.

There are many counterexamples that show a salutary effect of Hispanic immigration. Santa Ana, California, at 76 percent Latino the most heavily Spanish-speaking city of its size in the country, has cleaned up the seedy bars from its downtown area and replaced them with palm trees and benches, in large part thanks to a newly created business improvement district. Many homes in Santa Ana's wealthier Mexican neighborhoods sport exuberant roses and bougainvillea in their front yards, and students I spoke to there wanted to become lawyers, architects, and medical technicians. In predominantly Mexican East Los Angeles, housing prices are soaring along with the rest of the southern California housing market: a 1928 two-bedroom, one-bath bungalow with a lawn gone to seed was listed at $265,000 in April 2004. And in increasingly Hispanic South Central L.A., tiny bodegas selling milk, diapers, and piñatas are replacing liquor stores.

Yet a seemingly innocuous block in Santa Ana can host five to eight households dedicated to gangbanging or drug sales. A front yard may be relatively trash-free; inside the house, a different matter entirely, says Santa Ana cop Kevin Ruiz. "I've been to three houses just this week where they made a mountain of trash in the backyard or changed their baby's diaper by throwing it over the couch. They don't use the indoor plumbing, while letting their dogs go to the bathroom on the carpet." Ruiz drives by the modest tract home where his Mexican father, who worked in Orange County's farming industry, raised him in the 1950s. A car with a shattered windshield, a trailer, and a minivan sit in the backyard, surrounded by piles of junk and a mattress leaning on the garage door. "My mom taught us that even if you're poor, you should be neat," he says, shaking his head. Fifty-year-old men are still dressing like *cholos* (Chicano gangsters), Ruiz says, and fathers are ordering barbers to shave their young sons bald in good gang tradition.

Without prompting, Ruiz brings up the million-dollar question: "I don't see assimilation," he says. "They want to hold on [to Hispanic culture]." Ruiz thinks that today's Mexican immigrant is a "totally different kind of person" from those of the past. Some come with a chip on their shoulder toward the United States, he says, which they blame for the political and economic failure of their home countries. Rather than aggressively seizing the opportunities available to them, especially in education, they have learned to play the victim card, he thinks. Ruiz advocates a much more aggressive approach. "We need to explain, 'We'll help you assimilate up to a certain point, but then you have to take advantage of what's here.'"

Ruiz's observations will strike anyone who has hired eager Mexican and Central American workers as incredible. I pressed him repeatedly, insisting that Americans see Mexican immigrants as cheerful and hardworking, but he was adamant. "We're creating an underclass," he maintained.

Immigration optimists, ever ready to trumpet the benefits of today's immigration wave, have refused to acknowledge its costs. Foremost among them are skyrocketing gang crime and an expanding underclass. Until the country figures out how to reduce these costs, maintaining the current open-borders regime is folly. We should enforce our immigration laws and select immigrants on skills and likely upward mobility, not success in sneaking across the border.

6

HEATHER MAC DONALD

Hispanic Family Values?

Unless the life chances of children raised by single mothers suddenly improve, the explosive growth of the U.S. Hispanic population over the next couple of decades does not bode well for American social stability. Hispanic immigrants bring near–Third World levels of fertility to America, coupled with what were once thought to be First World levels of illegitimacy. (In fact, family breakdown is higher in many Hispanic countries than here.) Nearly half the children born to Hispanic mothers in the United States are born out of wedlock, a proportion that has been increasing rapidly with no signs of slowing down. Given what psychologists and sociologists now know about the much higher likelihood of social pathology among those who grow up in single-mother households, the Hispanic

baby boom is certain to produce more juvenile delinquents, more school failure, more welfare use, and more
teen pregnancy in the future.

The government social-services sector has already
latched on to this new client base; as the Hispanic population expands, so will the demands for a larger welfare
state. Since conservative open-borders advocates have yet
to acknowledge the facts of Hispanic family breakdown,
there is no way to know what their solution to it is. But
they had better come up with one quickly, because the
problem is here—and growing.

The dimensions of the Hispanic baby boom are startling. The Hispanic birthrate is twice as high as that of the
rest of the American population. That high fertility rate—
even more than unbounded levels of immigration—will
fuel the rapid Hispanic population boom in the coming
decades. By 2050 the Latino population will have tripled,
the Census Bureau projects. One in four Americans will be
Hispanic by mid-century, twice the current ratio. In states
such as California and Texas, Hispanics will be in the clear
majority. Nationally, whites will drop from near 70 percent
of the total population in 2000 to just half by 2050. Hispanics will account for 46 percent of the nation's added
population over the next two decades, the Pew Hispanic
Center reports.

But it's the fertility surge among *unwed* Hispanics that
should worry policymakers. Hispanic women have the
highest unmarried birthrate in the country—more than
three times that of whites and Asians, and nearly one and
a half times that of black women, according to the Centers

for Disease Control. Every 1,000 unmarried Hispanic women bore 92 children in 2003 (the latest year for which data exist), compared with 28 children for every 1,000 unmarried white women, 22 for every 1,000 unmarried Asian women, and 66 for every 1,000 unmarried black women. Forty-eight percent of all Hispanic births occurred outside of marriage in 2005, compared with 25 percent of white births and 16 percent of Asian births. Only the percentage of black out-of-wedlock births—68 percent—exceeds the Hispanic rate. But the black population will not triple over the next few decades.

As if the unmarried Hispanic birthrate weren't worrisome enough, it is increasing faster than among other groups. It jumped 5 percent from 2002 to 2003, whereas the rate for other unmarried women remained flat. Couple the high and increasing illegitimacy rate of Hispanics with their higher overall fertility rate, and you have a recipe for unstoppable family breakdown.

The only bright news in this demographic disaster story concerns teen births. Overall teen childbearing in the United States declined for the twelfth year in a row in 2003, having dropped by more than a third since 1991. Yet even here, Hispanics remain a cause for concern. The rate of childbirth for Mexican teenagers, who come from by far the largest and fastest-growing immigrant population, greatly outstrips every other group. The Mexican teen birthrate is 93 births per every 1,000 girls, compared with 27 births for every 1,000 white girls, 17 births for every 1,000 Asian girls, and 65 births for every 1,000 black girls. To put these numbers into international perspective, Japan's teen birthrate is 3.9, Italy's is 6.9, and France's is

10. Even though the outsize U.S. teen birthrate is dropping, it continues to inflict unnecessary costs on the country, to which Hispanics contribute disproportionately.

To grasp the reality behind those numbers, one need only talk to people working on the front lines of family breakdown. Social workers in southern California, the national epicenter for illegal Hispanic immigrants and their progeny, are in despair over the epidemic of single parenting. Not only has illegitimacy become perfectly acceptable, they say, but so has the resort to welfare and social services to cope with it.

Dr. Ana Sanchez delivers babies at St. Joseph's Hospital in the city of Orange, California, many of them to Hispanic teenagers. To her dismay, they view having a child at their age as normal. A recent patient just had her second baby at age seventeen; the baby's father is in jail. But what is "most alarming," Sanchez says, is that the "teens' parents view having babies outside of marriage as normal, too. A lot of the grandmothers are single as well; they never married, or they had successive partners. So the mom sends the message to her daughter that it's okay to have children out of wedlock."

Sanchez feels almost personally involved in the problem: "I'm Hispanic myself. I wish I could find out what the Asians are doing right." She guesses that Asian parents' passion for education inoculates their children against teen pregnancy and the underclass trap. "Hispanics are not picking that up like the Asian kids," she sighs.

Conservatives who support open borders are fond of invoking "Hispanic family values" as a benefit of unlimited Hispanic immigration. Marriage is clearly no longer one of those family values. But other kinds of traditional Hispanic values have survived—not all of them necessarily ideal in a modern economy, however. One of them is the importance of having children early and often. "It's considered almost a badge of honor for a young girl to have a baby," says Peggy Schulze of Chrysalis House, an adoption agency in Fresno. (Fresno has one of the highest teen pregnancy rates in California, typical of the state's heavily Hispanic farm districts.) It is almost impossible to persuade young single Hispanic mothers to give up their children for adoption, Schulze says. "The attitude is: 'How could you give away your baby?' I don't know how to break through."

The most powerful Hispanic family value—the tight-knit extended family—facilitates unwed child-rearing. A single mother's relatives often step in to make up for the absence of the baby's father. I asked Mona, a nineteen-year-old parishioner at St. Joseph's Church in Santa Ana, California, if she knew any single mothers. She laughed: "There are so many I can't even name them." Two of her cousins, aged twenty-five and nineteen, have children without having husbands. The situation didn't seem to trouble this churchgoer too much. "They'll be strong enough to raise them. It's totally okay with us," she said. "We're very close; we're there to support them. They'll do just fine."

As Mona's family suggests, out-of-wedlock child-rearing among Hispanics is by no means confined to the underclass. The St. Joseph's parishioners are precisely the churchgoing, blue-collar workers whom open-borders conservatives celebrate. Yet this community is as susceptible as any other to illegitimacy. Fifty-year-old Irma and her husband, Rafael, came legally from Mexico in the early 1970s. Rafael works in a meatpacking plant in Brea; they have raised five husky boys who attend church with them. Yet Irma's sister—a homemaker like herself, also married to a factory hand—is now the grandmother of two illegitimate children, one by each daughter. "I saw nothing in the way my sister and her husband raised her children to explain it," Irma says. "She gave them every-thing." One of the fathers of Irma's young nieces has four other children by a variety of different mothers. His con-struction wages are being garnished for child support, but he is otherwise not involved in raising his children.

The fathers of these illegitimate children are often problematic in even more troubling ways. Social workers report that the impregnators of younger Hispanic women are with some regularity their uncles, not necessarily seen as a bad thing by the mother's family. Alternatively, the fa-ther may be the boyfriend of the girl's mother, who then continues to stay with the grandmother. Older men seek out young girls in the belief that a virgin cannot get preg-nant during her first intercourse, and to avoid sexually transmitted diseases.

The tradition of starting families young and expanding them quickly can come into conflict with more modern American mores. Ron Storm, director of the Hillview Acres foster-care home in Chino, tells of a fifteen-year-old girl who was taken away from the twenty-one-year-old fa-ther of her child by a local child-welfare department. The boyfriend went to jail, charged with rape. But the girl's parents complained about the agency's interference, and eventually both the girl and her boyfriend ended up going back to Mexico, presumably to have more children. "At fifteen, as the Quinceañera tradition celebrates, you're considered ready for marriage," says Storm. Or at least for childbearing; the marriage part is disappearing.

But though older men continue to take advantage of younger women, the age gap between the mother and the father of an illegitimate child is quickly closing. Planned Parenthood of Orange and San Bernardino Counties tries to teach young fathers to take responsibility for their children. "We're seeing a lot more thirteen- and fourteen-year-old fathers," says Kathleen Collins, vice president of health education. The day before we spoke, Scott Montoya, an Orange County sheriff's deputy, arrested two fourteen-year-old boys who were bragging about having sexual relations with a cafeteria worker from an Olive Garden restaurant. "It's now all about getting girls pregnant when you're age fifteen," he says. One eighteen-year-old in the Planned Parenthood fathers' program has two children by two different girls and is having sex with five others, says health worker Jason Warner. "A lot of [the adolescent sexual behavior] has to do with getting respect from one's peers," observes Warner.

Normally the fathers, of whatever age, take off. "The father may already be married or in prison or doing drugs," says Amanda Gan, director of operations for Toby's House, a maternity home in Dana Point, California. Mona, the nineteen-year-old parishioner at St. Joseph's Church, says that the boys who impregnated her two cousins are "nowhere to be found." Her family knows them but doesn't know if they are working or in jail.

Two teen mothers at the Hillview Acres home represent the outer edge of Hispanic family dysfunction. Yet many aspects of their lives are typical. Although these teenagers' own mothers were unusually callous and irresponsible, the social milieu in which they were raised is not unusual.

Irene's round, full face makes her look younger than her fourteen years, certainly too young to be a mother. But her own mother's boyfriend repeatedly forced sex on her, with the mother's acquiescence. The result was Irene's baby, Luz. Baby Luz has an uncle her own age, Irene's new thirteen-month-old brother. Like Irene, Irene's mother had her first child at fourteen, and produced five more over the next sixteen years, all of whom went into foster care. Irene's father committed suicide before she was old enough to know him. The four fathers of her siblings are out of the picture too: one of them, the father of her seven-year-old brother and five-year-old sister, was deported back to Mexico after he showed up drunk for a visit with his children, in violation of his probation conditions.

Irene is serene and articulate—remarkably so, considering that in her peripatetic early life in Orange County she went to school maybe twice a week. She likes to sing and to read books that are sad, she says, especially books by Dave Pelzer, a child-abuse victim who has published three best-selling memoirs about his childhood trauma. She says she will never get married: "I don't want another man in my life. I don't want that experience again."

Eighteen-year-old Jessica at least escaped rape, but her family experiences were bad enough. The large-limbed young woman, whose long hair is pulled back tightly from her heart-shaped face, grew up in the predominantly

Hispanic farming community of Indio in the Coachella Valley. She started "partying hard" in fifth grade, she says—at around the same time her mother, separated from her father, began using drugs and going clubbing. By the eighth grade, Jessica and her mother were drinking and smoking marijuana together. Jessica's family had known her boyfriend's family since she was four; when she had her first child by him—she was fourteen and he was twenty-one—her mother declared philosophically that she had always known that it would happen. "It was okay with her, so long as he continued to give her drugs."

Jessica originally got pregnant to try to clean up her life, she says. "I knew what I was doing was not okay, so having a baby was a way for me to stop doing what I was doing. In that sense, the baby was planned." She has not used drugs since her first pregnancy, though she occasionally drinks. After her daughter was born, she went to live with her boyfriend in a filthy trailer without plumbing; they scrounged food from Dumpsters, despite the income from his illegal drug business. They planned to get married, but by the time she got pregnant again with a son, "We were having a lot of problems. We'd be holding hands, and he'd be looking at other girls. I didn't want him to touch me." Eventually, the county welfare agency removed her and put her in foster care with her two children.

Both Jessica and her caddish former boyfriend illustrate the evanescence of the celebrated Hispanic "family values." Her boyfriend's family could not be more traditional. Two years ago Jessica went back to Mexico to celebrate her boyfriend's parents' twenty-fifth wedding anniversary and the renewal of their wedding vows. Jessica's own mother got married at fifteen to her father, who was ten years her senior. Her father would not let his wife work; she was a "stay-at-home wife," Jessica says. But don't blame the move to the United States for the behavior of younger generations; the family crack-up is happening even faster in Latin America.

Jessica's mother may have been particularly negligent, but Jessica's experiences are not so radically different from those of her peers. "Everybody's having babies now," she says. "The Coachella Valley is filled with girls' pregnancies. Some girls live with their babies' dads; they consider them their husbands." These cohabiting relationships rarely last, however, and a new cohort of fatherless children goes out into the world.

Despite strong family support, the prevalence of single parenting among Hispanics is producing the inevitable slide into the welfare system. "The girls aren't marrying the guys, so they are married to the state," Dr. Sanchez observes. Hispanics now dominate the federal Women, Infants, and Children free-food program; Hispanic enrollment grew more than 25 percent from 1996 to 2002 while black enrollment dropped 12 percent and white enrollment dropped 6.5 percent. Illegal immigrants can get WIC and other welfare programs for their American-born children. If Congress follows President Bush's urging and grants amnesty to most of the eleven million illegal aliens in the country today, expect the welfare rolls to skyrocket as the parents themselves become eligible.

Amy Braun works for Mary's Shelter, a home for young single mothers who are homeless or in crisis, in Orange County, California. It has become "culturally okay" for the

Hispanic population to use the shelter and welfare system, Braun says. A case manager at a program for pregnant homeless women in the city of Orange observes the same acculturation to the social-services sector, with its grievance mongering and sense of victimhood. "I'll have women in my office on their fifth child, when the others have already been placed in foster care," says Anita Berry of Casa Teresa. "There's nothing shameful about having multiple children that you can't care for, and to be pregnant again, because then you can blame the system."

The consequences of family breakdown are now being passed from one generation to the next, in an echo of the black underclass. "The problems are deeper and wider," says Berry. "Now you're getting the second generation of foster care and group home residents. The dysfunction is multigenerational."

The social-services complex has responded with barely concealed enthusiasm to this new flood of clients. As Hispanic social problems increase, so will the government sector that ministers to them. In July a *New York Times* editorial, titled "Young Latinas and a Cry for Help," pointed out the elevated high school dropout rates and birthrates among Hispanic girls. A quarter of all Latinas are mothers by the age of twenty, reported the *Times*. With the usual melodrama that accompanies the pitch for more government services, the *Times* designated young Latinas as "endangered" in the same breath that it disclosed they are one of the fastest-growing segments of the population. "The time to help is now," said the *Times*—by which it means ratcheting up the taxpayer-subsidized social-work industry.

In response to the editorial, Carmen Barroso, regional director of International Planned Parenthood Federation / Western Hemisphere Region, proclaimed in a letter to the editor the "urgent need for health care providers, educators and advocates to join the sexual and reproductive health movement to ensure the fundamental right to services for young Latinas."

Wherever these "fundamental rights" might come from, Barroso's call nevertheless seems quite superfluous, since there is no shortage of taxpayer-funded "services" for troubled Latinas—or Latinos. The schools in California's San Joaquin Valley have day care for their students' babies, reports Peggy Schulze of Chrysalis House. "The girls get whatever they need—welfare, medical care." Advocates for young unwed moms in New York's South Bronx are likewise agitating for more day-care centers in high schools there, reports *El Diario / La Prensa*. A bill now in Congress, the Latina Adolescent Suicide Prevention Act, aims to channel $10 million to "culturally competent" social agencies to improve the self-esteem of Latina girls and to provide "support services" to their families and friends if they contemplate suicide.

The trendy "case management" concept, in which individual "cases" become the focal point around which a solar system of social workers revolves, has even reached heavily Hispanic elementary and middle schools. "We have a coordinator, who brings in a collaboration of agencies to deal with the issues that don't allow a student to meet his academic goals, such as domestic violence or drugs," explains Sylvia Rentria, director of the Family Resource Center at Berendo Middle School in Los Angeles.

"We can provide individual therapy." Rentria offers the same program at nearby Hoover Elementary School for up to one hundred students.

This July, Rentria launched a new session of Berendo's Violence Intervention Program for parents of children who are showing signs of gang involvement and other anti-social behavior. Ghady M., fifty-five and a *madre soltera* (single mother), like most of the mothers in the program, has been called in because her sixteen-year-old son Christian has been throwing gang signs at school, cutting half his classes, and ending up in the counseling office every day. The illegal Guatemalan is separated from her partner, who was *muy malo*, she says; he was probably responsible for her many missing teeth. (The detectives in the heavily Hispanic Rampart Division of the Los Angeles Police Department, which includes the Berendo School, spend inordinate amounts of time on domestic violence cases.) Although Ghady used to work in a factory on Broadway in downtown L.A.—often referred to as Little Mexico City—she now collects $580 in welfare payments and $270 in food stamps for her two American-born children.

Christian is a husky smart aleck in a big white T-shirt; his fashionably pomaded hair stands straight up. He goes to school but doesn't do homework, he grins; and though he is not in a gang, he says, he has friends who are. Keeping Ghady and Christian company at the Violence Intervention Program is Ghady's grandniece, Carrie, a lively ten-year-old. Carrie lives with her twenty-six-year-old mother but does not know her father, who also sired her twelve-year-old brother. Her five-year-old brother has a different father.

Yet for all these markers of social dysfunction, father-less Hispanic families differ from the black underclass in one significant way: many of the mothers and the absent fathers work, even despite growing welfare use. The former boyfriend of Jessica, the eighteen-year-old mother at the Hillview Acres foster home, works in construction and moonlights on insulation jobs; whether he still deals drugs is unknown. Jessica is postponing joining her father in Texas until she finishes high school, because once she moves in with him, she will feel obligated to get a job to help the family finances. The mother of Hillview's fourteen-year-old Irene used to fix soda machines in Anaheim, California, though she got fired because she was lazy, Irene says. Now, under court compulsion, she works in a Lunchables factory in Santa Ana, a condition of getting her children back from foster care. The eighteen-year-old lothario and father of two, whom Planned Parenthood's Jason Warner is trying to counsel, works at a pet store. The mother of Carrie, the vivacious ten-year-old sitting in on Berendo Middle School's Violence Intervention Program, makes pizza at a Papa John's pizza outlet.

How these two value systems—a lingering work ethic and underclass mating norms—will interact in the future is anyone's guess. Orange County sheriff's deputy Montoya says that the older Hispanic generation's work ethic is fast disappearing among the gangbanging youngsters whom he sees. "Now it's all about fast money, drugs, and sex." It may be that the willingness to work will plummet along with marriage rates, leading to even greater social problems than are now rife among Hispanics. Or it may be that the two contrasting practices will remain on parallel tracks, creating a new kind of underclass: a culture that tolerates free-floating men who impregnate women and leave, like the vast majority of black men, yet who still labor in the noncriminal economy. The question is whether, if the disposition to work remains relatively strong, a working parent will inoculate his or her illegitimate children against the worst degradations that plague black ghettos.

From an intellectual standpoint, this is a fascinating social experiment, one that academicians are—predictably—not attuned to. But the consequences will be more than intellectual: they may severely strain the social fabric. Nevertheless it is an experiment that we seem destined to see to its end. Tisha Roberts, a supervisor at an Orange County, California, institution that assists children in foster care, has given up hope that the illegitimacy rate will taper off. "It's going to continue to grow," she says, "until we can put birth control in the water."

7

HEATHER MAC DONALD

Mexico's
Undiplomatic Diplomats

It's a strain being a Mexican diplomat in the United States these days, as the plaintive expression on Mario Velázquez-Suárez's dignified features suggests. Diplomacy may be the art of lying for one's country, but Mexican diplomacy requires taking that art to virtuosic heights. Sitting in his expansive office in Mexico's Los Angeles consulate, Deputy Consul General Velázquez-Suárez gamely insists that he and his peers observe the diplomatic duty not to interfere in America's internal affairs, including immigration matters. "Immigration is an internal discussion," he says. "We have to respect that regardless of whether it pleases us."

Well, at least one part of the deputy consul general's statement is true: immigration is an "internal discussion." The decision about who can enter and permanently reside in a country is central to its identity. The rest of his statement, though, is utterly false. Mexican officials here and abroad are involved in a massive and almost daily interference in American sovereignty. The dozens of illegals milling in the consulate's courtyard as Velázquez-Suárez speaks, as well as the millions more radiating outward from Los Angeles across the country, are not a naturally occurring phenomenon, like the tides. They are there thanks in part to Mexico's efforts to get them into the United States in violation of American law and to normalize their status once here in violation of the popular will. Mexican consulates are engineering a backdoor amnesty for their illegal migrants and trying to discredit American immigration enforcement—activities clearly beyond diplomatic bounds.

Mexico's governing class is not content simply to unload the victims of its failed policies on the United States, however. It also tries to ensure that migrants retain allegiance to *La Patria*, so as to preserve the $24 billion in remittances they send to Mexico each year. Mexican leaders have thus directed their nation's U.S. consulates to spread Mexican culture into American schools and communities. Given the American public's swelling anger about illegal immigration, it's past time for Washington to tell Mexico to cease interfering and for the Bush administration to start enforcing the law.

Just how shameless is Mexico in promoting illegal entry into the United States? For starters, it publishes a comic book–style guide on breaching the border safely and evading detection once across. Mexico's foreign ministry distributes the *Guía del Migrante Mexicano* (Guide for the Mexican Migrant) in Mexico; Mexican consulates along the border hand it out in the United States. The pamphlet is also available on the website of the Instituto de los Mexicanos en el Exterior, or IME (Institute for Mexicans Abroad), the cabinet-level agency that promotes *Mexicanismo* in the United States.

Nodding to U.S. law, the guide does briefly remind readers that "mechanisms for legal entry" into the United States exist and are the surest way to get in. But the book primarily consists of "practical advice" for entering illegally: *do* drink salt water and cross when the heat is lowest; *don't* wear heavy clothing when fording a river. *Do* keep your coyote in sight; *don't* send your children across the border with strangers—a Mexican variation on the usual parental advice. And *don't* "throw rocks or objects at officials or at patrols since this is considered a provocation by those officials." (This last piece of advice clearly hasn't taken hold: attacks on the border patrol have steadily increased in number and viciousness.)

The guide's recommendations on how to avoid detection once in the United States are equally no-nonsense: *do* keep your daily routines stable, to avoid calling attention to yourself; *don't* engage in domestic violence—the Marvel comic–type illustration shows a macho man, biceps bulging, socking a woman a big one in the jaw. *Don't* drink and drive because it could result in deportation if you're arrested.

Mexico backs up the publication with serious resources for the collective assault on the border. An elite law-enforcement team called Grupo Beta protects illegal migrants, as they sneak into the United States, from corrupt Mexican officials and criminals—essentially pitting two types of Mexican lawlessness against each other. Grupo Beta currently maintains aid stations for Mexicans crossing the desert. In April 2005 it worked with Mexican federal and Sonoran state police to help steer illegal aliens away from Arizona border spots patrolled by Minutemen border-enforcement volunteers—demagogically denounced by President Vicente Fox as "migrant-hunting groups."

Disseminating information about how to evade a host country's laws is not typical consular activity. Consulates exist to promote the commercial interests of their nations abroad and to help nationals if they have lost passports, gotten robbed, or fallen ill. If a national gets arrested, consular officials may visit him in jail to ensure that his treatment meets minimum human rights standards. Consuls aren't supposed to connive in breaking a host country's laws or intervene in its internal affairs.

The border-breaking guide is just the tip of the iceberg of Mexican meddling, however. After 9/11, Vicente Fox's government realized that the immigration amnesty it had expected from President Bush was on hold. So it came up with the second-best thing: a de facto amnesty, at the heart of which is something called the *matricula consular* card.

Mexican consulates, like those of other countries, have traditionally offered consular cards to their nationals abroad for registration purposes, in case they disappear.

In practice, few Mexicans bothered to obtain them. After 9/11, though, officials at Los Pinos (the Mexican presidential residence) ordered their consulates to promote the card as a way for illegals to obtain privileges that the United States usually reserves for legal residents. The consulates started aggressively lobbying American government officials and banks to accept *matriculas* as valid IDs for driver's licenses, checking accounts, mortgage lending, and other benefits.

The only type of Mexican who would need such identification is an illegal one; legal aliens already have sufficient documentation to get driver's licenses or bank accounts. Predictably, the IDs flew off the shelf—more than 4.7 million since 2000. Every day illegals seeking *matriculas* swamp the consulates. Every seat and place to stand in the modest, white stucco Santa Ana, California, consulate was filled one morning this July, most of the people there seeking the two hundred or so *matriculas* that the consulate issues per day.

The Mexican government knows just how subversive its *matricula* effort is. A consulate's right to issue such a card to its nationals is indisputable; where the Mexican diplomats push the envelope is in lobbying governments to adopt it as an American ID. In announcing the normalization-through-the-*matricula* push, then–foreign minister Jorge Castañeda was characteristically blunt: "We are already giving instructions to our consulates that they begin propagating militant activities—if you will—in their communities."

And yet, Mexico's consuls comically pretend they know nothing of their countrymen's immigration violations and wouldn't possibly interfere with America's response even if they did. "Our formal policy is not to ask the immigration status, because we don't have anything to do with that," explains the outspoken consul for Santa Ana, Luis Miguel Ortiz Haro Amieva, speaking in his narrow office above the consular reception area. "Our services don't have anything to do with immigration status," he says, implausibly.

This pose gets more challenging all the time, because legal immigration from Mexico has basically stopped. Eighty percent of all Mexicans who arrived in the United States over the last decade crossed the border furtively, a rate that has only increased of late. These illegal arrivals now outnumber legal Mexicans in the United States. And the more the disabilities of illegal status diminish, the greater the future flow of illegals will be.

You would think that an ID obtainable simply by showing Mexican nationality would not elicit fraud from Mexican nationals themselves. But Santa Ana consul Ortiz Haro whips out a stack of counterfeit Mexican voting cards and birth certificates that the consulate has confiscated from *matricula* applicants, bought at document bazaars like Los Angeles's MacArthur Park. Some applicants can't be bothered to get their real Mexican documents; others want to avoid extortion by relatives who demand payment to send those documents, says Ortiz Haro. He is confident, however, that the consulate can spot all fakes and verify, say, a birth certificate from the remotest Mexican peasant village. The FBI demurs: it opposes the use of the *matriculas* as American IDs because the consulates lack adequate safeguards against counterfeiting.

The consuls' protestations of ignorance about their nationals' immigration statuses are particularly far-fetched when it comes to tracking down missing border breakers. "If someone crosses but hasn't been heard from," says Santa Ana protective-services director Mildret Avila, speaking in Spanish and carefully avoiding details of that crossing, "the family will come to us and say: 'Our brother was supposed to arrive but hasn't come.' We'll contact the consulates all along the border—in San Diego, Calexico, Denver, and Phoenix, who will ask the Immigration and Customs Enforcement and check the hospitals and prisons to try to find him."

What about inquiring with the coyotes? "We never hear from them," Avila says. "We don't know who the family pays; the coyotes just disappear." Note that at this point in the interview, Avila is implicitly acknowledging that the Mexican nationals in question are illegal. Not for long, though. Why don't you tell someone who is in the country illegally that he should return to Mexico and get permission to enter? I ask. "We don't know if someone has papers or not." You could ask, couldn't you? "Yes."

Now, arguably, individual consuls aren't obligated to police compliance with American law—that responsibility lies with American authorities. But Mexico's disrespect for the law regarding its illegal migrants actually begins on its side of the border. Mexico's own regulations require that all exits from the country go through established crossing points. Decades ago, Mexico enforced that rule. Now, any Mexican can cross wherever he wants. A few years ago the governor of Baja California proposed reviving the law as a means of preventing desert-crossing deaths. He swiftly found himself denounced for kowtowing to the Americans, writes former U.S. ambassador to Mexico Jeffrey Davidow in his book *The Bear and the Porcupine*. The proposal died.

Mexicans view migration to the United States as a fundamental human right, says Davidow; no laws should stop it, they believe. In addition, nearly 60 percent of Mexican respondents polled by Zogby in 2001 said that the southwestern United States really belongs to Mexico. Only 28 percent disagreed.

Mexican consuls denounce any U.S. law-enforcement effort against illegal immigration as biased and inhumane. For the moment they still tolerate deportations if officials pick up the illegal Mexican right at the border and promptly set him down on the other side—whence he can try again the next day. Once in the United States, however, an illegal gains untouchable status, in the consuls' view.

In 2002 the Denver consulate planted sympathetic stories in the *Denver Post* about an illegal Mexican high school student, Jesus Apodaca, who could not afford out-of-state tuition to Colorado colleges. Consulate spokesman Mario Hernández lobbied Colorado legislators to award in-state tuition to Apodaca. When the stories ran, Republican congressman Tom Tancredo, a vocal opponent of illegal immigration, suggested that Apodaca might more properly be deported. Such impertinence was more than Hernández could bear. "This is an arrogant use of power," he declared. "I don't think Mr. Tancredo realizes what he is doing to this family, which is already vulnerable." The family's "vulnerability," of course, was wholly of its own making.

Colorado governor Bill Owens disagreed with the consulate's contention that the state should treat Apodaca as a legal resident for the purpose of state-subsidized tuition. He didn't dare suggest that Apodaca actually be—gasp!—deported. Nevertheless, in retaliation for Owens's opposition to a tuition grant, consul Leticia Calzada undiplomatically urged Mexican tourists to boycott Colorado and visit Wyoming instead.

No less righteously angry was San Diego's consul following the border patrol's arrest of a family of illegal aliens near the consulate. The family was on its way to pick up *matriculas*. Objected Consul General Rudolfo Figueroa: "We feel outraged over the way [the arrest] was handled. This was an act of bad faith." The consul filed a formal complaint with the border patrol; the Mexican embassy in Washington demanded—and got—a formal investigation into the matter. Mexico's foreign ministry said the arrests violated a "gentleman's agreement" that its consulates could carry out their duties without the presence of law enforcement. The ministry might ponder why there should be any conflict between Mexican consular duties and the rule of law.

Boston's consul general sharply protested the arrest of several illegal Mexicans in April 2005. Ipswich, New Hampshire, police chief W. Garrett Chamberlain had grown frustrated with the federal government's refusal to take custody of illegal aliens whom his deputies reported to immigration agents. So he charged a Mexican illegal for criminal trespass—for being in a place without legal authority. A chief in a nearby town followed suit. Mexican officials went berserk: if this legal move succeeded—and police chiefs across the country immediately declared interest in using it—it would breach the nationwide sanctuary for Mexico's illegals.

Pulling out all the stops, the Mexican government paid for the defendants' legal representation—another departure from traditional diplomatic practice, which forbids interference in a host country's judicial process unless it is patently unfair. Boston consul general Porfirio Thierry Muñoz Ledo declared the Ipswich trial "legally invalid, discriminatory and a violation of human rights." Yet the New Hampshire chiefs weren't using the law against the defendants because they were Mexican but because they were illegal. No legal Mexican need worry about arrest for trespass or for violations of the immigration law. Mexico's campaign against immigration enforcement, however, equates being Mexican with being illegal—a presumption that the country would undoubtedly label racist if an American articulated it.

For the moment, Mexican illegals inside the border are safely insulated from enforcement. A New Hampshire judge rejected the Ipswich indictment this August, ruling that local police departments may not use trespass law against immigration violators. Since the federal authorities virtually refuse to arrest immigration violators, and since most big cities forbid their police to inquire into immigration status, the nation remains one big sanctuary for illegals.

Mexico's consuls go even further in undermining U.S. border law. They're evolving a "disparate impact" theory that holds that any police action is invalid if it falls upon illegal Mexicans, even if that action has nothing to do with immigration. In July 2005 the Mexican consul general in New York City, Arturo Sarukhan, lambasted Suffolk County, Long Island, officials for evicting more than a hundred illegal aliens whose dangerously overcrowded housing violated fire and safety codes. The code enforcement constituted a "vilif[ication]" of the Mexicans, Sarukhan said, and inflamed community "tensions." Policing fire and safety codes is a core function of local government—unless it interferes with an illegal Mexican, in the New York consul general's view. He might note that the "tensions" in Long Island aren't due to the Suffolk County government but to the continuing influx of Latin Americans flouting American law.

Quick to defend individual illegals, the consuls just as energetically fight legislative measures to reclaim the border. Voters nationwide have lost patience with the federal government's indifference to illegal immigration, which imposes crippling costs on local schools, hospitals, and jails that must serve or incarcerate thousands of illegal students, patients, and gangbangers. Californians in 1994 launched the first protest against this unjustifiable tax burden by passing Proposition 187, banning illegals from collecting welfare. Mexico's Los Angeles consulate swiftly joined forces with southern California open-borders groups to invalidate the law, even giving the Coalition for Humane Immigrant Rights in Los Angeles a computer and database to help build a case against the proposition. Mexican action against 187 apparently extended to Mexico as well. After a federal judge struck down the initiative in

1998, Los Angeles councilman (now mayor) Antonio Villaraigosa credited Mexican president Ernesto Zedillo with helping to undermine it.

In November 2004, Arizona voters passed Proposition 200 over the strenuous protests of the Phoenix consul general, who sent out press releases urging Hispanics to vote against it. The proposition merely reaffirmed existing law that requires proof of citizenship to vote and to receive certain welfare benefits. After the law passed, Mexico's foreign minister threatened to bring suit in international tribunals for this egregious human rights violation, and the Phoenix consulate supported the Mexican-American Legal Defense and Education Fund's federal lawsuit against the proposition.

Back in Mexico, politicians blast any hint that American legislators might obstruct illegals' free pass. In May, Congress passed the Real ID Act, which rendered driver's licenses issued to illegal aliens inadmissible for aircraft boarding and at other federal security checkpoints. Mexico's interior minister, Santiago Creel, lashed out: the law is "absurd, it is not understandable in light of any criteria," he said. In fact the law was quite understandable: after 9/11, Congress wanted to make sure that federal authorities had properly vetted aliens given access to sensitive areas, such as airplanes. Creel, however, dismissed U.S. security concerns; the fact that the illegals "send their remittances and also benefit the Mexican economy," he declared, was far more important.

Former foreign minister Jorge Castañeda showed similar contempt for America's terrorism worries this July. He haughtily told the Senate Foreign Relations Committee that Mexico would cooperate with the United States on future security matters only if Washington granted amnesty to illegal Mexican aliens. Military-to-military cooperation is "very, very sensitive" to Mexicans, explained Castañeda. Americans' sensitivity to widespread contempt for its sovereignty—well, that's not even worth paying attention to.

The gall of Mexican officials does not end with the push for illegal entry. After demanding that we educate their surplus citizens, give those citizens food stamps, deliver their babies, provide them with doctors and hospital beds, and police their neighborhoods, the Mexican government also expects us to help preserve their loyalty to Mexico.

Since 1990, Mexico has embarked on a series of initiatives to import Mexican culture into the United States. Mexico's five-year development plan in 1995 announced that the "Mexican nation extends beyond . . . its border"— into the United States. Accordingly, the government would "strengthen solidarity programs with the Mexican communities abroad by emphasizing their Mexican roots, and supporting literacy programs in Spanish and the teaching of the history, values, and traditions of our country."

The current launching pad for these educational sallies is the Instituto de los Mexicanos en el Exterior. The IME directs several programs aimed at American schools. Each of Mexico's 47 consulates in the United States (a number that expands nearly every year) has a mandate to introduce Mexican textbooks into schools with significant Hispanic populations. The Mexican consulate in Los Angeles showered nearly 100,000 textbooks on 1,500 schools in the

Los Angeles Unified School District this year alone. Hundreds of thousands more have gone to school districts across the country, which pay only shipping charges. Showing admirable follow-up skills, the consulates try to ensure that students actually read the books. L.A. consulate reps, for instance, return to schools that have the books and ask questions. "We test the students," explains Mireya Magaña Gálvez, a consul press attaché. "We ask the students: 'What are you reading about now?' We try to repeat and repeat."

Like most explanations offered for Mexican involvement in American cultural matters, the justification for the textbook initiative is tortured. "If people are living in the U.S., of course they need to become excellent citizens of this place," says Magaña Gálvez. "If we can help in their education, they will understand better." But if the goal is American assimilation, why take a detour through Mexican history? "We must talk about Mexican history," she explains. "Our history is very rich, very intensive. It's important to know that history. The students will feel proud to become Americans if they feel proud of their country."

Immigrants have often tried to hold on to their native traditions, but not until recently did anyone expect American schools to help them do so. And it is hard to see how studying Mexican history from a Mexican perspective helps forge an American identity. The Mexican sixth-grade history book, for example, celebrates the "heroism and sacrifice" of the Mexican troops who fought the Americans during the Mexican War in 1846–1848. But "all the sacrifices and heroism of the Mexican people were use-less," recounts the chronicle. The "Mexican people saw the enemy flag wave at the National Palace." The war's conse-quences were "disastrous," notes the primer: "To end the occupation, Mexico was obligated to sign the treaty of Guadeloupe-Hidalgo," by which the country lost half its territory.

This narrative is accurate and rather tame by Mexico's usual anti-American standards. But a student in the United States could easily find himself confused about his allegiances. Is his country Mexico or the United States? Study exercises that include discovering "what happened to your territory when the U.S. invaded" don't clarify things. The textbook concludes by celebrating Mexican patriotic symbols: the flag, the currency, and the national anthem. "We love our country because it is ours," the primer says.

Mexican consulates also push for bilingual education in American schools, with the same odd logic with which they defend teaching Mexican history: teaching in Span-ish, they say, will make students better English speakers. In this nonsensical claim, the Mexican officials are of course at one with the American bilingual-education es-tablishment. No surprise, then, that the National Associa-tion of Bilingual Educators has conferred awards on Mexico's education ministry for its support of Spanish-language instruction or that the association is represented on the IME's advisory council.

The IME also supplies adult-education materials in Spanish language and culture to community colleges and public libraries, and expects them to provide the space, teachers, and technology for distance-learning courses. "The Glendale library [in the Los Angeles suburbs] is beautiful," enthuses the L.A. consulate's Magaña Gálvez. It has converted half its space to a Spanish-language center using Mexico's course materials, she says.

Yet does this Spanish-language project actually result in the acquisition of English? I put this question to Socorro Torres Sarmiento, the community affairs coordinator in the Santa Ana consulate. She dodged the question: "It's difficult to do English at the same time," she said. In other words, probably not.

The consulates appear to regard local opposition to their bilingual agenda with bemused contempt. Santa Ana's consul, Ortiz Haro, says conspiratorially of his host city: "Here, we are living 'just English' in the schools. We have problems with some school districts [in Orange County], especially in Santa Ana. This high school district is involved in a lot of political issues, I think they have a very conservative point of view about education." Of course, what Ortiz Haro calls "political issues" is simply the school board's effort to follow the mandate of Proposition 227, the 1998 California voter initiative that sought to curtail bilingual ed in California schools.

But the consuls don't easily give up in fighting to preserve and increase the use of Spanish in the United States. Torres Sarmiento, Santa Ana's community affairs coordinator, visits Orange County schools to promote a Mexican government–sponsored drawing contest, *Éste Es Mi México* (This Is My Mexico). When Torres Sarmiento speaks to the students in Spanish, she—predictably—receives resistance: "The teacher says, 'You need to speak English, because we're not allowed to speak Spanish.'" Undaunted, Torres Sarmiento reminds the children not to forget their Spanish—valid advice, but irrelevant to the school context, where teaching Mexican students English should be the paramount concern.

The contest that Torres Sarmiento is promoting is another device to reinforce a sense of Mexicanness in students. It asks them to draw pictures expressing the "history, culture, natural resources, people, or traditional holidays [of] our beloved and beautiful country." Winners get a trip to Mexico City at the Mexican government's expense. Here again—in conservative Orange County, California, at least—some schools are skittish about sponsoring a Mexican government–designed program. Torres Sarmiento responds that embracing Mexican culture is vital for students' self-esteem. In her school visits for the contest, she asks students if they know who the Aztecs were.

"Unfortunately," she says, "they often don't." But if the students are to succeed in the United States, a more relevant question might be: Do you know who the Pilgrims were?

The U.S. Department of Education, no foe of multiculturalism, collaborates with some of Mexico's education initiatives. It helps bring hundreds of Mexican teachers to U.S. schools for part of the school year or during the summer—and not just to Mexican population centers like Los Angeles but also to recent outposts in the Mexican diaspora, such as Green Forest, Arkansas. The visitors suggest methods by which American teachers can incorporate

Mexican dance, songs, and history, especially the indigenous cultures of the Toltec, Mayas, and Mistecas, into their lessons, notes Edda Caraballo, director of Migrant Education for the California Department of Education.

Such devotion to other countries' folkways would be unimpeachable if students overflowed with knowledge of America's history. As survey after survey has found, however, American students know next to nothing about their country's past. Only one-third of seniors at elite colleges could pick out the general at the battle of Yorktown from among William Sherman, Ulysses Grant, Douglas MacArthur, and George Washington, according to a 2000 American Council of Trustees and Alumni survey.

A huge proportion of the Mexican students receiving school-based training in Mexicanismo are illegal, making American help in preserving an alien culture all the more remarkable. The burden of illegal immigration has fallen heaviest on California, where one-quarter of the nation's illegals live and where one-quarter of the students don't speak English. The Anaheim school district in Orange County recently floated a $132 million bond measure to meet the costs of educating illegal aliens and their children. Santa Ana consul Ortiz Haro laughs as he recounts that Anaheim school administrators had wanted to bill Mexico for the cost of educating its illegal exports—a perfectly sensible idea that strikes him as ludicrous. Concern with border breaking is, to a Mexican consulate, well, just a little uncouth.

The audacity of Mexico's interference in U.S. immigration policy stands in sharp contrast to Mexico's own jealous sense of sovereignty. It is difficult to imagine a country touchier about interference in its domestic affairs or less tolerant of immigrants. In 2002, for example, Mexico deported a dozen American college students (all in the country legally) who had joined a protest in Mexico City against a planned airport. Such participation, said Mexico, constituted illegal domestic interference. (It would be interesting to know how many Mexican students—legal and illegal—have participated with impunity in demonstrations in the United States against American immigration and educational policies.) During his confirmation hearings, U.S. Ambassador Jeffrey Davidow said innocuously that the United States would encourage high participation in Mexico's 2000 presidential election. A magazine editor rebuked him for "intromission in Mexico's internal affairs." Davidow didn't even dare visit the troubled state of Chiapas early in his tenure, knowing that the press would condemn it as illegal meddling.

Imagine if U.S. diplomats yowled constantly about Mexico's unfair policies toward illegal Americans. Mexico would expel them instantly. In the summer of 2005, U.S. Ambassador to Mexico Tony Garza closed the U.S. consulate in Nuevo Laredo after a particularly bloody period of drug violence that included the assassination of the town's police chief. Garza admitted to a reporter that he shut the consulate "in part" to punish Mexico for its failure to control the mayhem. Such measured language, in response to a public threat, provoked a sharp correction from Mexico's deputy foreign secretary, Gerónimo Gutiérrez. Garza's words, fumed Gutiérrez, do "not correspond to the role of an ambassador."

But Mexican diplomats in the United States often express far harsher, and ad hominem, political judgments, with little regard for protocol. Santa Ana consul Ortiz Haro does not conceal his disdain in observing that California Propositions 187 and 209 (banning racial preferences), as well as the Minuteman Project, originated in Orange County. "We have six Congressmen here; five are Republicans. That would not be so bad," he adds magnanimously, "except for the kind of Republican: [Dana] Rohrabacher, [Ed] Royce; these are friends of Tancredo, who says we need the military on the border."

Mexican politicians are even starting to allege that American responses to illegal immigration in the United States are a violation of Mexico's sovereignty. In August 2005, New Mexico governor Bill Richardson declared a state of emergency in four counties bordering Mexico because of violence and devastation wrought by trafficking in aliens and drugs. City council members from the Mexican city of Ciudad Juárez branded Richardson's declaration an interference in Mexico's domestic affairs.

Mexico's own immigration policies are the exact opposite of what it relentlessly advocates in the United States. Its entry permits favor scientists, technicians, teachers of underrepresented disciplines, and others likely to contribute to "national progress." Immigrants may enter only through established ports and at designated times. Anyone not presenting the proper documentation and health certificates won't get in; the transportation company that brought him must pay his return costs. Foreigners who do not "strictly comply" with the entry conditions will face deportation. Steve Royster, who worked in the American consulate in Mexico from 1999 to 2001, presided over several deportations of Americans who had overstayed their visas. "They were given a choice: accept deportation or go to jail," he says.

Providing full college tuition or all-expenses-paid secondary and primary education for illegal American students in Mexico? Unthinkable. Until recently, U.S.-born children of Mexican parents weren't even allowed to enroll in Mexican public schools, reserved for Mexican citizens only. The parents would have to bribe officials for Mexican birth certificates for their kids. (The 1998 change in the Mexican constitution to allow dual nationality now makes enrollment by U.S.-born Mexicans possible.) "We're not friendly with immigrants; that's a big difference with the speech we have here with American schools," admits a Mexican diplomat.

What about textbooks to propagate American culture in Mexico? They would provoke an uprising against Yanqui imperialism. When President Ernesto Zedillo tried in the 1990s merely to revise Mexican textbooks to acknowledge contemporary cooperation between the United States and Mexico, he found himself denounced as a traitor. The revisions went nowhere.

Mexico's border police have reportedly engaged in rapes, robberies, and beatings of illegal aliens from Central and South America on their way to the United States. Yet compared with the extensive immigrant-advocacy network in the United States, few pressure groups exist in Mexico to protest such treatment. If Americans run afoul of Mexico's border police, watch out. In 1996 the Mexican police beat and shot in the back a teenage American girl who had led them on a high-speed chase in Tijuana. No one in the United States or Mexico raised a fuss, at least publicly.

Contrast that incident with another that occurred in the United States a few months earlier. A vanload of Mexican illegals in California had fled from the border patrol and the Riverside County deputies, throwing metal bars and beer cans at their pursuers and sideswiping cars to divert attention. When the van stopped, the deputies caught two of the fleeing occupants and beat them. Mexico's foreign ministry turned the beating into an international human rights incident, attributing it to "discriminatory attitudes that lead to institutional violence." Mexican diplomats formally protested to state and federal officials, and helped the two beaten Mexicans file multimillion-dollar lawsuits against the deputies and Riverside County. The State Department abjectly apologized and promised to set the FBI and Justice Department on the case. Had American authorities responded to the Tijuana beating with comparable anger and PR savvy, the Mexican backlash would have been fierce.

And if American politicians, presiding over a grotesquely mismanaged economy and the exodus of millions of citizens, adopted the grandiose rhetoric of Mexican politicians, they would be a laughingstock from one end of Mexico to the other. Heralding the creation of the IME and its parent agency, the National Council for Mexican Communities Abroad, President Vicente Fox argued that these bodies were necessary to "defend the human, civil, and labor rights [of Mexican migrants] more effectively, as well as to protect them against adversity or arbitrariness." The idea that the *American* government represents a heightened threat of "arbitrariness," compared with the corrupt Mexican bureaucracy, or that Mexico needs to protect its refugees from "adversity" abroad when it can't provide them with a reasonable living at home, is simply delusional.

Mexico's struggle to hold the hearts of its fleeing countrymen has worked. Mexican migrants have maintained a strong nationalism, exhibited through the "unfailing celebration of Mexican national, religious, and regional holidays, the conspicuous displays of patriotic symbols in Mexican neighborhoods and businesses, and in the low naturalization rate," writes University of California professor Luis Eduardo Guarnizo. In the last decade, the rate of naturalization among legal Mexican immigrants did improve, in response to the 1996 welfare-reform law, which reduced welfare eligibility for noncitizen immigrants, and to Mexico's authorization of dual nationality in 1998 (not exactly ideal motives for becoming citizens). The rate is still well below the immigrant norm, however. In 2001 just 34 percent of eligible Mexicans became citizens, compared with 58 percent of other Latin Americans, 67 percent of Asians, and 65 percent of Canadians and Europeans.

The Mexican government will push to control as much U.S. immigration policy as it can get away with. It's up to American officials to stop such interference, but the Bush administration simply winks at foreign attacks on immigration laws that it itself refuses to enforce. President

Bush should worry less about upsetting his friends at Los Pinos and more about listening to the American people: illegal immigration, they believe, is an affront to the rule of law and a threat to American security. It can and must be stopped.

———————————————————————

8
———

VICTOR DAVIS HANSON

Mexifornia, Five Years Later

In the Spring 2002 issue of *City Journal* I wrote an essay about growing up in the central San Joaquin Valley and witnessing firsthand, especially over the last twenty years, the ill effects of illegal immigration (*City Journal*'s editors chose the title of the piece: "Do We Want Mexifornia?"). Controversy over my blunt assessment of the disaster of illegal immigration from Mexico led to an expanded memoir, *Mexifornia*, published the following year by Encounter Press.

Mexifornia came out during the ultimately successful campaign to recall California governor Gray Davis in autumn 2003. A popular public gripe was that the embattled governor had appeased both employers and the more radical Hispanic politicians of the California legislature on illegal immigration. And indeed Davis had signed legislation allowing driver's licenses for illegal aliens that both houses of state government had passed. So it was no wonder that the book sometimes found its way into both the low and high forms of the political debate. On the Internet a close facsimile of a California driver's license circulated, with a picture of a Mexican bandit (the gifted actor Alfonso Bedoya of *The Treasure of the Sierra Madre*), together with a demeaning height (five feet, four inches), weight ("too much"), and sex ("mucho") given. "Mexifornia" was emblazoned across the top where "California" usually is stamped on the license.

In such a polarized climate, heated debates and several radio interviews followed, often with the query, "Why did you have to write this book?" The Left saw the book's arguments and its title—*Mexifornia* was originally a term of approbation used by activists buoyed by California's changing demography—as unduly harsh to newcomers from Mexico. The Right saw the book as long-overdue attention to a scandal ignored by the mainstream Republican party.

Fast-forward nearly five years, and the national climate has radically changed, so much so that the arguments of *Mexifornia*—close the borders, return to the melting pot, offer earned citizenship to most aliens of long residence in exchange for acceptance of English and American culture—seem tame today, if not passé. In 2002, when I wrote the original *City Journal* essay, no one thought the U.S. Congress would vote to erect a wall. Today there is rumbling that the signed legislation entails only 700 miles of fencing instead of spanning the entire 1,950-mile border.

Deportation was once an unimaginable response to the problem of the eleven million here illegally. Now its practicality, rather than its morality, appears the keener point of contention. And the concerted effort by Chicano activists to drive from popular parlance the descriptive term "illegal alien" in favor of the politically correct but imprecise and often misleading "undocumented worker" has largely failed. Similar efforts to demonize opponents of open borders as "anti-immigrant" or "nativist" have had only a marginal effect in stifling debate, as has the deliberate effort to blur illegal and legal immigration. The old utopian talk of a new borderless zone of dual cultures, spreading on both sides of a disappearing boundary, has given way to a reexamination of NAFTA and its facilitation of greater cross-border flows of goods, services—and illegal aliens and drugs.

So why has the controversy over illegal immigration moved so markedly to the right?

We return always to the question of numbers. While it is true that no one knows exactly how many are here illegally from Mexico and Latin America, both sides in the debate often accept as reasonable estimates of 11 to 12 million illegals—with an additional 500,000 to 1 million arriving each year. Given porous borders, such guesses about the number of illegal aliens in the United States are outdated almost as soon as they are published. It is plausible, then, that there may be an additional 3 to 4 million illegal aliens here who were not here when the *City Journal* "Mexifornia" piece appeared.

The result of such staggering numbers is that aliens now don't just cluster in the American Southwest but frequently appear at Home Depot parking lots in the Midwest, emergency rooms in New England, and construction sites in the Carolinas, making illegal immigration an American, rather than a mere Californian or Arizonan, concern.

Indeed, we forget how numbers are at the crux of the entire debate over illegal immigration. In the 1970s perhaps a few million illegals resided in the United States, and their unassimilated presence went largely unnoticed. Most Americans felt that the formidable powers of integration and popular culture would continue to incorporate any distinctive ethnic enclave, as they had so successfully done with the past generations that arrived en masse from Europe, Asia, and Latin America. But when more than ten million fled Mexico in little over a decade—the great majority poor, without English, job skills, a high school education, and legality—entire apartheid communities in the American Southwest began springing up.

During the heyday of multiculturalism and political correctness in the 1980s, the response of us, the hosts, to this novel challenge was not to insist upon the traditional assimilation of the newcomer but rather to accommodate the illegal alien with official Spanish-language documents, bilingual education, and ethnic boosterism in our media, politics, and education. These responses only encouraged more illegals to come, on the guarantee that their material life could be better and yet their culture unchanged in the United States. We now see the results. Los Angeles is today the second-largest Mexican city in the world; one of every ten Mexican nationals resides in the United States, the vast majority illegally.

Since *Mexifornia* appeared, the debate also no longer splits along liberal/conservative, Republican/Democrat, or even white/brown fault lines. Instead, class considerations more often divide Americans on the issue. The majority of middle-class and poor whites, Asians, African Americans, and Hispanics wish to close the borders. They see few advantages to cheap service labor, since they are not so likely to need it to mow their lawns, watch their kids, or clean their houses. Because the less well-off eat out less often, use hotels infrequently, and don't periodically remodel their homes, the advantages to the economy of inexpensive, off-the-books illegal-alien labor again are not so apparent.

But the downside surely is apparent. Truck drivers, carpenters, janitors, and gardeners—unlike lawyers, doctors, actors, writers, and professors—correctly feel that their jobs are threatened, or at least their wages lowered, by cheaper rival workers from Oaxaca or Jalisco. And Americans who live in communities where thousands of illegal aliens have arrived en masse more likely lack the money to move when Spanish-speaking students flood the schools and gangs proliferate. Poorer Americans of all ethnic backgrounds take for granted that poverty provides no exemption from mastering English, so they wonder why the same is not true for incoming Mexican nationals. Less than a mile from my home is a former farmhouse whose new owner moved in several stationary Winnebagos, propane tanks, and outdoor cooking facilities—and apparently four or five entire families rent such facilities right outside his back door. Dozens live where a single family used to—a common sight in rural California that reifies illegal immigration in a way that books and essays do not.

The problem with all this is that our now-spurned laws were originally intended to ensure an (admittedly thin) veneer of civilization over innate chaos—roads full of drivers who have passed a minimum test to ensure they are not a threat to others; single-family residence zoning to ensure that there are adequate sewer, garbage, and water services for all; periodic county inspections to ensure that untethered dogs are licensed and free of disease and that housing is wired and plumbed properly to prevent mayhem; and a consensus on school taxes to ensure that there are enough teachers and classrooms for such sudden spikes in student populations.

All these now-neglected or forgotten rules proved costly to the taxpayer. In my own experience, the slow progress made in rural California since the 1950s of my youth—in which the county inspected our farm's rural dwellings, eliminated the once-ubiquitous rural outhouse, shut down substandard housing, and fined violators in hopes of providing a uniform humane standard of residence for all rural residents—has been abandoned in just a few years of laissez-faire policy toward illegal aliens. My own neighborhood is reverting to conditions common about 1950, but with the insult of far higher tax rates added to the injury of nonexistent enforcement of once-comprehensive statutes. The government's attitude at all levels is to punish the dutiful citizen's misdemeanors while ignoring the alien's felony, on the logic that the former will at least comply while the latter either cannot or will not.

Fairness about who is allowed into the United States is another issue that reflects class divides—especially when almost 70 percent of all immigrants, legal and illegal, arrive from Mexico alone. Asians, for example, are puzzled as to why their relatives wait years for official approval to enter the United States, while Mexican nationals come across the border illegally, counting on serial amnesties to obtain citizenship.

These class divisions cut both ways, and they help explain the anomaly of the *Wall Street Journal* op-ed page mandarins echoing the arguments of the elite Chicano studies professors. Both tend to ridicule the far less affluent Minutemen and English-only activists, in part because they do not experience firsthand the problems associated with illegal immigration but instead find millions of aliens grist for their own contrasting agendas. Indeed, every time an alien crosses the border legally, fluent in English and with a high school diploma, the La Raza industry and the corporate farm or construction company alike most likely lose a constituent.

The ripples of September 11—whether seen in the arrests of dozens of potential saboteurs here in America or the terrorist bombings abroad in Madrid and London—remind Americans that their present enemies can do us harm only if they can first somehow enter the United States. Again, it makes little sense to screen tourists, inspect cargo containers, and check the passenger lists of incoming flights when our border with an untrustworthy Mexico remains porous. While it may be true that the opponents of illegal immigration have used the post–September 11 fear of terrorism to further their own agenda of closing the border with Mexico, they are absolutely correct that presently the best way for jihadist cells to cross into the United States is overland from the south.

Other foreign developments have also steered the debate ever more rightward. In the last decade the United States has clearly seen the wages of sectarianism and ethnic chauvinism abroad. The unraveling of Yugoslavia into Croatian, Serbian, and Albanian sects followed the Hutu-Tutsi bloodbath in Rwanda. And now almost daily we hear of Pashtun-Tajik-Uzbek hatred among the multiplicity of warring clans in Afghanistan and the daily mayhem among Kurds, Shiites, and Sunnis in Iraq. Why—when we are spending blood and treasure abroad to encourage the melting pot and national unity—would anyone wish to contribute to tribalism or foster the roots of such ethnic separatism here in the United States?

Moreover, all during the 1990s, blue-state America offered up the European Union as the proper postmodern antidote to the United States. But just as we have recoiled from the EU's statist and undemocratic tendencies—which have resulted in popular dissatisfaction, sluggish economic growth, high unemployment, falling demography, and unsustainable entitlement commitments—so, too, have its unassimilated Muslim minorities served as another canary in the mine. The riots in France, the support for jihadism among Pakistanis in London, and the demands of Islamists in Scandinavia, Germany, and the Netherlands do not encourage Americans to let in more poor Mexican illegal immigrants with loud agendas, or to embrace the multicultural salad bowl over their own distinctive melting pot.

Then there were the April–May 2006 demonstrations here in the United States, when nearly half a million protesters took to the streets of our largest cities, from Chicago to Los Angeles. Previously, naive Americans had considered that their own discussions over border security and immigration were in their own hands. And while Chicano rights organizations and employer lobbyists were often vehement in their efforts to keep the border open, illegal aliens themselves used to be mostly quiet about our internal legal debates.

In contrast, in spring 2006 Americans witnessed millions of illegal aliens who not only were unapologetic about their illegal status but were demanding that their hosts accommodate their own political grievances, from providing driver's licenses to full amnesty. The largest demonstrations—held on May Day, with thousands of protesters waving Mexican flags and bearing placards depicting the Communist insurrectionist Che Guevara—only confirmed to most Americans that illegal immigration was out of control and beginning to become politicized along the lines of Latin American radicalism. I chronicled in *Mexifornia* the anomaly of angry protesters waving the flag of the country they vehemently did not wish to return to, but now the evening news beamed these images to millions. In short, the radical socialism of Latin America, seething in the angry millions who flocked to support Venezuela's Hugo Chávez, Bolivia's Evo Morales, and Mexico's Andrés López Obrador, had now seemingly been imported into our own largest cities.

Turmoil in areas of Mexico that send many illegal aliens to the United States is especially worrisome. Recently, for example, almost the entire state of Oaxaca was in near-open revolt over efforts to force the resignation of provincial governor Ulises Ruiz Ortiz. There was wide-spread lawlessness, vigilantism, and at times the complete breakdown of order. All this feeds the growing perception that illegal aliens increasingly are arriving not merely as economic refugees but as political dissidents who don't hesitate to take to the streets here to demand social justice, as they did back home.

More important still, Oaxaca's troubles cast doubt on the conventional wisdom that illegal immigration is a safety valve that allows Mexico critical time to get its house in order. Perhaps the opposite is true: some of the areas, such as Oaxaca, that send the greatest number of illegal aliens to the United States, still experience the greatest social tensions—in part because of the familial disruption and social chaos that result when adult males flee and depopulated communities consequently become captive to foreign remittances.

Two further issues have persuaded Americans to close the borders: the attitude of the Mexican government and the problems with first-generation native-born children of illegal aliens.

Worker remittances sent back to Mexico now earn it precious American dollars equal to the revenue from 500,000 barrels daily of exported oil. In short, Mexico cannot afford to lose its second-largest source of hard currency and will do almost anything to ensure its continuance. When Mexico City publishes comic books advising its own citizens how best to cross the Rio Grande, Americans take offense. Not only does Mexico brazenly wish to undermine American law to subsidize its own failures, but it also assumes that those who flee northward are among its least educated, departing without much ability to read beyond the comic-book level.

We are also learning not only that Mexico wants its expatriates' cash—and its nationals lobbying for Mexican interests—once they are safely away from their motherland; we are also discovering that Mexico doesn't have much concern about the welfare of its citizens abroad in America. The conservative estimate of $15 billion sent home comes always at the expense of low-paid Mexicans toiling here, who must live in impoverished circumstances if they are to send substantial portions of their wages home to Mexico. (And it comes as well at the expense of American taxpayers, providing health care and food subsidies in efforts to offer a safety net to cash-strapped illegal aliens.) So it is not just that Mexico exports its own citizens but that it does so with the expectation that they are serfs of a sort, who, like the helots of old, surrender much of the earnings of their toil to their distant masters.

But even more grotesquely, in the last five years the Mexican real-estate market has boomed on the Baja California peninsula. Once Mexico grasped that its own unspoiled coast was highly desirable for wealthy expatriate Americans as a continuation of the prized but crowded Santa Barbara–San Diego seaside corridor, it began to reform its real estate market, making the necessary changes in property and title law, and it welcomed with open arms cash-laden subdividers looking to come south. This is sound economics, but examine the ethical message: Mexico City will send the United States millions of its own illiterate and poor whom it will neither feed nor provide with even modest housing, but at the same time it welcomes thousands of Americans with cash to build expensive seaside second homes.

Of course the ultimate solution to the illegal immigration debacle is for Mexican society to bring itself up to the levels of affluence found in the United States by embracing market reforms of the sort we have seen in South Korea, Taiwan, and China. But rarely do Mexican supporters of such globalization, or their sympathetic counterparts in the United States, see the proliferation of a Wal-Mart or Starbucks down south in such terms. Rather, to them American consumerism and investment in Mexico suggest only an owed reciprocity of sentiment: Why should Americans get mad about Mexican illegals coming north when our own crass culture, with its blaring neon signs in English, spreads southward? In such morally equivalent arguments, it is never mentioned that Americanization occurs legally and brings capital while Mexicanization comes about by illegal means and is driven by poverty.

At the same time focus has turned more to the U.S.-born children of Mexican illegal immigrants, in whom illegitimacy, school dropout rates, and criminal activity have risen to such levels that no longer can we simply dismiss Mexican immigration as resembling the more problematic but eventually successful Italian model of a century ago. Then, large numbers of southern European Catholics, most without capital and education, arrived en masse from Italy and Sicily, lived in ethnic enclaves, and for decades lagged behind the majority population in educational achievement, income, and avoidance of crime—before achieving financial parity as well as full assimilation and intermarriage. Since 1990 the number of poor Mexican Americans has climbed 52 percent, a figure that skewed U.S. poverty rates. Billions of dollars spent on our own poor will not improve our poverty statistics when one million of the world's poorest cross our border each year. The number of impoverished black children has dropped 17 percent in the last sixteen years, but the number of Hispanic poor has gone up 43 percent. We don't like to talk of illegitimacy, but here again the ripples of illegal immigration reach the U.S.-born generation. Half of births to Hispanic Americans were illegitimate, 42 percent higher than the general rate of the American population. Illegitimacy is higher in general in Mexico than in the United States, but the force multiplier of illegal status, lack of English, and an absence of higher education means that the children of Mexican immigrants have illegitimacy rates even higher than those found in either Mexico or the United States.

Education levels reveal the same dismal pattern— nearly half of all Hispanics are not graduating from high school in four years. And the more Hispanic a school district becomes, the greater level of failure for Hispanic students. In the Los Angeles district, 73 percent Hispanic, 60 percent of the students are not graduating. But the real tragedy is that, of those Hispanics who do graduate, only about one in five will have completed a high school curriculum that qualifies for college enrollment. That partly helps explain why at many campuses of the California State University system, almost half the incoming class must first take remedial education. Fewer than 10 percent of those who identify themselves as Hispanic have graduated from college with a bachelor's degree. I found that teaching Latin to first-generation Mexican Americans and illegal aliens was valuable not so much as an introduction to the ancient world but as their first experience with remedial English grammar.

Meanwhile, almost one in three Mexican-American males between the ages of eighteen and twenty-four recently reported being arrested, one in five has been jailed, and fifteen thousand illegal aliens are currently in the California penal system.

Statistics like these have changed the debate radically. While politicians and academics assured the public that illegal aliens came here only to work and would quickly assume an American identity, the public's own ad hoc and empirical observations of vast problems with crime, illiteracy, and illegitimacy have now been confirmed by hard data. Ever since the influx of illegals into our quiet valley became a flood, I have had five drivers leave the road, plow into my vineyard, and abandon their cars, without evidence of either registration or insurance. On each occasion I have seen them simply walk or run away from the scene of thousands of dollars in damage. Similarly, an intoxicated driver who ran a stop sign hit my car broadside and then fled the scene. Our farmhouse in the Central Valley has been broken into three times. We used to have an open yard; now it is walled, with steel gates on the driveway. Such anecdotes have become common currency in the American Southwest. Ridiculed by elites as evidence of prejudice, these stories, statistical studies now show, reflect hard fact.

The growing national discomfort over illegal immigration more than four years after "Mexifornia" first appeared in *City Journal* is not only apparent in the rightward shift of the debate but also in the absence of any new arguments for open borders—while the old arguments, Americans are finally concluding, really do erode the law, reward the cynical here and abroad, and needlessly divide Americans along class, political, and ethnic lines.

STEVEN MALANGA

The Right Immigration Policy

We Americans are having the wrong immigration debate, couched in the wrong terms. Those who oppose open borders, and especially unlimited flows of low-skilled workers from Mexico, are accused of being anti-immigration. Anyone who doubts that it's good for America to have an amnesty for illegal immigrants and a "guest worker" program that will produce even more low-wage, low-skilled immigration is quickly branded a modern-day nativist and Know-Nothing.

But it's possible to oppose all those things and still support healthy levels of immigration. The right debate should be about what kind of immigrants America should be admitting. It should ask how immigration can best benefit our economy and citizens. Countries with booming economies, countries that are, like the United States, immigrant magnets—Australia and Ireland, for instance—have set their immigration priorities in precisely this way, creating much more rational systems than ours. Managed as part of our broader economic policy, immigration can provide America with badly needed skills, boost productivity, and raise our living standard.

But we'll never get to an immigration system that serves our national interest until we stop debating the issue in terms set down fifty years ago.

Open-borders advocates are right to say that immigration made America great: we are indeed, as the cliché goes, a nation of immigrants. But it's important to understand why previous generations of immigrants succeeded in America, how they helped the country grow, and how today's immigration differs. The popular image of the 24 million who came during the first great migration, from the 1880s to the 1920s, is that they were Europe's "tired" and "poor" masses, desperately escaping political or religious persecution and stagnant economies, making their way here with a few threadbare possessions. But what's forgotten is that many were also skilled workers. A 1998 National Academy of Sciences study noted that the immigrant workers of that era generally met or exceeded the skill levels of the native-born population, providing America's workforce with a powerful boost just when the country was metamorphosing from an agrarian into an industrial economy.

Even though nativists agitated to bar these Southern and Eastern European immigrants because they were not Anglo-Saxon, it was not until after World War I that Congress—stunned by the growing radicalism of European workers in the wake of the Russian Revolution and by postwar turmoil in Europe—finally enacted immigration quotas based on national origin, with the purpose of shifting the balance of immigration back to Northern European countries. Those quotas helped cut immigration in half, though it was the depression that truly ended the great migration, turning America into a net exporter of emigrants during the 1930s, as 60 percent of those who came for a better life left when the economy soured, according to the National Academy of Sciences study.

For forty years the 1920s laws largely governed and limited immigration (with certain exceptions for refugees), until new legislation in the mid-1960s unintentionally precipitated the waves of low-skilled immigration that we now see. The new law, which the Kennedy administration introduced as a civil rights measure that would abolish the supposedly racist national-origins quotas and give preference to immigrants with family members already in the United States, would, supporters claimed, make U.S. immigration policy fairer but would have little impact on levels of migration. Instead the law had far-reaching unanticipated consequences, dramatically increasing the immigration of unskilled workers from poorer countries. From the 1950s to the 1970s, immigration from Asia soared tenfold, and from Africa fivefold, while newcomers from Central and South America doubled.

Today, when success in our economy requires ever more skills and education, the vast majority of immigrants arrive without the skills or the education to fit in easily anywhere except at the lowest economic rung. A study by Harvard economists George Borjas and Lawrence Katz noted that 63 percent of Mexican immigrants are high school dropouts who on average earn 53 percent less than native workers when they enter the United States. Because such immigrants start so far behind, this income gap can persist for decades, research shows. Moreover, because so much of today's immigration now hails from just a few countries (Mexican immigrants now represent 30 percent of America's foreign-born population, whereas no two ethnic groups during the first great migration accounted for 25 percent), immigrants increasingly group in insulated communities of their own, where their children adopt the cultural attributes of their home country rather than those of America. High school graduation rates among the American-born children of Hispanic immigrants are much lower than the average in the rest of the native-born population, while census surveys have begun to record growing numbers of native-born Hispanics who don't have English-language proficiency—nearly three million in the 2005 American Community Survey.

Meanwhile the benefits of so much low-wage immigration to our economy are minimal and increasingly outweighed by the costs. Low-skilled immigrant workers have crowded into service jobs that do little to make America more competitive internationally or more productive: they deliver our pizzas, cut our lawns, wash our cars. True, these immigrants push down prices of services for middle-class Americans, but they also depress the wages of low-skilled native-born workers, according to Borjas and Katz, and recent studies show that they probably raise the unemployment levels of native-born blacks and Hispanics. Not surprisingly, a 1997 study by economists for the National Academy of Sciences estimated the net benefits of immigration at only $10 billion in our $8 trillion economy, while the next year an NAS study of the social costs of immigration reported that in California each native-born family paid nearly $1,200 more in taxes to support government services that went to immigrants. Those costs will only grow as the number of immigrants in America increases. The Heritage Foundation's Robert Rector has estimated that each immigrant high school dropout will cost U.S. taxpayers $85,000 over his lifetime. Enacting amnesty for illegals already here, as well as creating a new guest-worker program, Rector calculates, would eventually add some $46 billion a year in social costs—including welfare—to the federal government.

As America has grappled with its increasingly costly immigration, other developed countries have transformed the way they think about immigration, placing more emphasis on economic considerations and the cultural capital that immigrants bring with them. Like the United States, Australia for much of its history had an immigration policy based on race and nationality. But the country's slowing economic performance in the mid-1980s prompted the government to rethink its policies. The result: a skills-based immigration approach that welcomes workers who have the experience and training in jobs the economy needs, posted on the so-called Australian Migration Occupations in Demand List. The new policy recognizes that from an economic point of view, not all workers are equal. Among the most sought-after workers in recent years have been accountants, nurses, and tradesmen, including mechanics and electricians. To qualify for a visa to work at a job on the MODL, potential immigrants must show that they have the right skills, workforce experience, English-language proficiency, and age. Those over forty-five cannot gain permanent skills-based residency because their contribution to the Australian economy will be too brief to offset the social costs they will impose on society.

The policy has led to a dramatic shift in the nature of Australian immigration. Whereas in 1993 70 percent of all immigration was based on family relations, today 70 percent of Australia's permanent visas go to skilled workers. As a result, Australian immigrants do far better than American immigrants. A 2006 study by the Australian Productivity Commission (roughly the equivalent of our Government Accountability Office) shows that on average Australian immigrants earn about 6 percent more than the median income of the native-born population, because immigrants typically have higher levels of education and skills. Even Australian immigrants in the country for less than five years earn 4 percent more than the native-born. By contrast, because the preponderance of low-skilled workers pulls the average down, American immigrants earn 20 percent less than the median native-born worker. The shift toward welcoming more skilled immigration has prompted the Australian government to declare that it is winning the worldwide contest for better-trained workers: "We are beating the U.S., Canada, and New Zealand," Australia's former immigration minister (and now attorney general), Philip Ruddock, has boasted.

Other countries have adopted a similar skills-based approach. Canada, for instance, gives would-be immigrants additional "points" for advanced educational degrees and for knowing both French and English. But because the country does not try to match immigrants to specific jobs shortages the way Australia does, some highly educated immigrants—especially those from Asian and Latin American countries, according to a recent study—find it difficult to get jobs in their professional fields once they arrive in Canada. Moreover, Canada's emphasis on education without reference to what the labor market needs has prompted frustration in industries like construction, which has shortages of skilled workers. As a result, immigrants in Canada, on average, earn less than native-born workers.

Ireland has taken yet a third approach, letting employers select candidates for visas and prohibiting immigrants from shifting jobs once they arrive, unless they can find another business to sponsor them. Ireland's approach aims to manage surges of immigration that result from the dramatic growth of the country's economy, thanks to the heroic tax cuts and deregulation of the early 1990s. From being an exporter of emigrants for much of its history, Ireland became a net importer of immigrants as capital rushed in from around the world and unemployment rates fell from nearly 16 percent to about 5 percent by the end of the decade.

As newcomers poured into the country, Ireland reshaped its policy to prevent unskilled workers from flooding its labor markets. So that employers don't import immigrants in occupations where workers are already plentiful, aiming to drive down wages, Ireland won't grant visas in job categories for which market surveys deem the labor supply adequate. Virtually all the jobs for which the country currently won't grant work visas—from hotel workers to retail salespeople to clerical staff—are low-skilled. Ireland requires that employers try to fill vacancies in those jobs from Ireland itself or with workers from other EU countries, who can migrate to Ireland without restriction. As a result, 25 percent of the country's immigration hails from EU members Latvia, Lithuania, and Poland.

The other half of a sound immigration policy is to eliminate the magnet effect of modern welfare programs. Developed countries uniformly prohibit illegal aliens from receiving social benefits, and many restrict those benefits for legals too. Australia, for instance, prohibits legal immigrants from participating in social programs for two years. Immigrants in Canada who qualify for a skilled-worker visa must show a bank account of at least $9,420 (Canadian) before entering the country, to ensure that they won't become an immediate burden on the welfare system. Canadian residents who want to sponsor a relative under the country's family reunification program must also prove that they have the resources to support the immigrant. (America makes a similar demand that those who sponsor immigrants pledge to support them in case of need, but it doesn't require sponsors to honor the promise.)

Similarly, Ireland restricts legal immigrants from receiving many social welfare benefits. Moreover, in 2004 Irish citizens voted to amend their constitution to stop granting automatic citizenship to children born in the country of foreign parents, after widespread reports that immigrants were flying to Dublin to give birth because

Irish law allowed the parents to take up residence in the country with their citizen-child thereafter. Now at least one parent must be legally resident in Ireland for three of the four years before the child's birth for their baby to become a citizen.

Welfare-benefit restrictions are an acknowledgment that the economic calculus of immigration has changed dramatically. Before the welfare state, which developed countries have all embraced to some degree, immigrants came to a country like the United States because its free-enterprise system gave them an opportunity to succeed—but not a guarantee. Those who failed often returned home, and one reason why studies showed that immigrants did so well during the first great migration is that those who came were the most enterprising and those who stayed were the most skilled at adapting to our economy.

But today the modern welfare state has turned the self-selection process upside down, offering immigrants from very poor countries incentives to come to America and sponge off the taxpayers, reaping where they did not sow. Today's immigrants are more than twice as likely to use government programs as native-born Americans. As Nobel laureate Milton Friedman said, "It's just obvious that you can't have free immigration and a welfare state."

The experience of other countries provides clear guidelines for the kind of immigration policy the United States should adopt. And as early as the 1990s, a bipartisan congressional commission on immigration reform sketched out some of the reform's essential principles. It concluded, based on recommendations from leading economists, that the United States should stop admitting unskilled workers into the country, because there was no widespread need for them, and that such immigration was not "in the national interest." It further recommended that the country should not institute any guest-worker programs for industries like agriculture, because such programs "effectively expand rural poverty" by importing large numbers of very low-paid workers. The commission also recommended that the United States reduce total immigration levels by one-third to assimilate better those who *are* coming and to reduce the costs of immigration on our society. Although the Republican-controlled Congress and President Clinton initially accepted the commission's work, both parties backed off when political opposition arose from an unusual alliance of business interests, open-borders ideologues, ethnic and racial activists, and Mexican politicians.

Nonetheless, the United States should now try to push through the reforms that the commission's economists suggested and that the experience of other nations has proven to be beneficial. The first step is to acknowledge that our family unification policy, our current immigration law's centerpiece, not only does not serve our economy but goes way beyond preserving the nuclear family. Current law allows not only the spouses and minor children of permanent residents and American citizens—both native-born and naturalized—to come here, but also their adult sons and daughters as well as the parents and adult siblings of citizens. This chain of relations accounts for some 600,000 legal visas a year and has prompted a backlog of some 4 million visa applicants. By restricting the family unification category to the spouses and minor children of citizens, the United States could cut family-unification visas in half.

Reducing family visas would allow for a shift toward skills-based immigration without increasing the number of newcomers. To determine what kinds of workers would receive skills-based visas, the United States would shift away from its current system in which those visas—totaling only 77,000 last year—now almost entirely go to highly educated workers, such as technology specialists, whom companies request, but not to skilled tradesmen who might also be in short supply. Under a revised system, while companies could continue to request visas for workers they need, the United States would also award visas based on the model of Australia's Migration Occupation Demands List, compiled through labor-market surveys. In Australia that list currently is heavily weighted toward trades like automotive electricians, boilermakers, machinists, toolmakers, and welders. The U.S. Labor Department's list of more than 200 of the fastest-growing job categories includes many similar trades, but potential immigrants with those skills have virtually no way of getting into the country legally unless they are high on the family reunification list. An immigration policy designed to strengthen the U.S. economy would bump workers in such fast-growing trade categories to the top of visa lists. By reorienting immigration toward more skilled workers, the United States would probably diversify its immigration flow and could eliminate its so-called diversity category, which grants 50,000 visas a year to winners of a lottery.

For these changes to have much impact, the nation will have to get much tougher on illegal immigration, now about a quarter of all immigration and almost entirely unskilled. Although hardening the border is important, the real key is to lessen the economic incentives to sneak into the United States by ensuring that businesses don't hire workers they know to be illegal and that government doesn't provide them with services and benefits. The 1990s commission on immigration reform recommended establishing a national database for employers to verify the Social Security numbers of their workers. Now is the time to do it.

Although eliminating economic incentives will stem the flow of illegals and send many home, stricter enforcement also means more deportations. Open-borders proponents argue that the United States can never deport all of the estimated 11 million immigrants here—something it would never be necessary to do—but it is nevertheless a fundamental principle of policing that failing to enforce laws spurs more illegal activity while stepped-up enforcement discourages it. Canada has followed this policy, beefing up its Border Services Agency and increasing deportations, estimated to rise to about 10,000 this year in an illegal population of about 200,000. By comparison, the United States deports some 50,000 annually out of its 11 million–strong illegal population.

Reducing economic incentives, of course, entails eliminating government benefits to illegals. Although the federal government bans illegal aliens from receiving many benefits, several states and cities have made themselves immigrant havens by providing government services through a "don't ask, don't tell" policy. New York City, for instance, offers immigrants, regardless of their status, such benefits as government-sponsored health insurance, preventive medical care, and counseling programs. Some states have moved to ensure that illegals receive in-state tuition discounts to state colleges, even though out-of-state American citizens don't qualify for those discounts. Although the states administer many of these services, they are often supported by funding from the federal government, which should move to withhold all funds from state and municipal programs that openly provide services to illegals. Immigration is a federal issue, and individual states and cities cannot have their own policies.

Finally, the United States should begin a debate on whether to stop granting citizenship to everyone born here of foreign parents—a right that no EU country grants. The right springs from the first sentence of the Fourteenth Amendment, passed after the Civil War to ensure that states did not deny citizenship to former slaves. The framers of the amendment did not intend it to apply to the children of noncitizens who happen to be born here, though the Supreme Court has interpreted it that way, because its language does not specifically exclude those children. America has never had a discussion about whether we want to extend citizenship to these children, and now is the time to begin that conversation. Currently the children of our 11 million illegal aliens automatically become citizens with the right to apply for visas for their parents and siblings to immigrate here legally. And they have the right to government benefits, including "child-only" welfare payments, which vary greatly by state but can amount to up to $500 a month for two children in California.

Reordering our immigration policies in this way would give a big boost to our economy. Not only do skilled workers create more wealth than unskilled ones, but studies consistently show that economies make more productive use of skilled workers, since businesses invest more in new machinery and equipment when skilled labor is available. And, of course, better-paid, skilled workers are unlikely to need taxpayer-funded social programs. Meanwhile lower-income Americans, who now suffer from the depressing effect that unskilled immigration has on their wages, would also benefit, because their pay would rise.

Such a policy shift would also diversify our stream of newcomers, as it did Australia's, and help ensure that immigrants continue to assimilate economically and culturally. Today's family-based immigration policy has resulted in millions of Hispanic immigrants living in insulated, unassimilated ethnic communities where their children retain the characteristics of their immigrant culture, including out-of-wedlock childbearing and a low valuation of education. A reformed immigration policy would result in fewer such enclaves, where the ethnic capital handed down by one generation to the next is out of step with what it takes to succeed in the American economy.

America's current immigration policy doesn't satisfy the majority of our own citizens, who say in polls by a two-to-one margin that they would like to see immigration levels reduced. Our immigration law is also out of step with how other countries that are economic powerhouses have ordered their own policy. Our debate revolves around a law that is an anachronism, formulated fifty years ago to sanitize U.S. policy of any hints of racism or nativism and resulting in far-reaching, unintended negative consequences. Now it's time to move the discussion into the twenty-first century.

Index

Advocacy groups, 91–92; and immigration, 43
Affirmative action, 28
Afghanistan, 162
Aguilera, Guadalupe, 64
American culture: transformation of, 70
Americanization: vs. Mexicanization, 166
American Southwest, 157; apartheid communities in, 158
Amnesty, 3, 7, 59; border control, undermining of, 74; and deportation, 61; and entitlement, 54, 58; national sovereignty, challenge to, 53; opponents of, 53; proponents of, 52, 54, 70, 73

Anti-sovereignty movement, 58
Apodaca, Jesus, 138, 139
Arenas, Valentino, 67, 102
Arizona, 73; and Proposition 200, 142
Arkansas, 43
Asia: immigration from, 35, 46, 172
Assimilation, 8, 9, 24, 49, 97; among Hispanic population, 69; and Mexican Americans, 108; and Mexican immigrants, 71; and multiculturalism, 11–12
Austin (Tex.), 76
Australia, 183; immigration policy of, 50, 171, 176; and Migration Occupation in

A NOTE ON THE AUTHORS

Heather Mac Donald, a nonpracticing lawyer, is a senior fellow at the Manhattan Institute and author of *The Burden of Bad Ideas* and *Are Cops Racist*? She is a contributing editor of *City Journal*; her writings have also appeared in the *New York Times*, the *Washington Post*, the *Wall Street Journal*, and *The New Republic*, among other publications.

Victor Davis Hanson, a senior fellow at the Hoover Institution, is the author of *A War Like No Other*, *Between War and Peace*, and *Mexifornia*, among other books. His syndicated column appears in newspapers throughout the country.

Steven Malanga, who has also written *The New New Left*, is senior editor of *City Journal* and a senior fellow at the Manhattan Institute specializing in urban economies, business communities, and public policy.

Myron Magnet, former editor of *City Journal*, is the author of *The Dream and the Nightmare* and *Dickens and the Social Order*, and editor of *The Millennial City*, *Modern Sex*, and *What Makes Charity Work*?